# In Search of Emily

## Journeys From Japan to Amherst

*Masako Takeda*

Quale Press

Emily Dickinson's poems are reprinted by permission of the publishers and the Trustees of Amherst College from *The Poems of Emily Dickinson*, Thomas H. Johnson, ed., Cambridge, Mass.: The Belknap Press of Harvard University Press, Copyright © 1951, 1955, 1979, 1983 by the President and Fellows of Harvard College.

Emily Dickinson's letters are reprinted by permission of the publishers from *The Letters of Emily Dickinson*, Thomas H. Johnson, ed., Cambridge, Mass.: The Belknap Press of Harvard University Press, Copyright © 1958, 1986 by the President and Fellows of Harvard College.

Helen Hunt Jackson's letter to Emily Dickinson (L444a) is quoted by permission of The Houghton Library, Harvard University *MS Am 1118.4 (L51)* © The President and Fellows of Harvard College. Helen Hunt Jackson's letter to Emily Dickinson (L476a) is quoted by permission of The Houghton Library, Harvard University © The President and Fellows of Harvard College. T.W. Higginson's letter to his wife (L342a) is quoted courtesy of the Trustees of the Boston Library/Rare Books Department.

"The Evergreens" was first published in a different version in the *Massachusetts Review*, Vol. XXXIV, No. 4, Winter 1993–94.

Copyright © 2005 by Masako Takeda

Cover: "Masako's Journeys," collage (8.75" x 12.5") by Gian Lombardo

ISBN: 0-9744503-3-2 trade paperback edition

LCCN: 2005922600

Quale Press
www.quale.com

# In Search of Emily

Journeys From Japan
to Amherst

# Contents

Preface  *vii*
Introduction  *ix*
Discovering Emily  *1*
Amherst, 1986  *11*
Emily's Amherst  *18*
An American Education  *31*
Amherst's Poet-Philosopher  *36*
Learning the Language  *43*
Philadelphia and the Depth of Emily's Heart  *49*
Emily's Letters  *56*
Boston, 1987  *63*
Museums and Meditations  *73*
The Art of Calligraphy  *79*
Amherst, 1993  *84*
A Literary Landscape  *89*
Celebrating Emily  *98*
Simsbury High School  *103*
Inspired by Emily  *112*
The Belles of Amherst  *121*

*In Search of Emily*

The Evergreens    126
A Dancing Star    137
The Ever-Changing World of Emily    142
Epilogue    153

# Preface

THIS BOOK IS THE FRUIT OF MY LOVE OF EMILY DICKINSON'S POETRY, from which blossoms an abiding curiosity of her life, time and locale. This book is the sum and body of my visits to the United States in search of Emily. The bulk of my time visiting the United States was spent in three stays: from August 1986 to June 1987, from April 1993 to March 1994, and from March to September 2000. I have also made shorter visits, including one in 1990 for the National Endowment for the Humanities Summer Institute and almost every summer for the annual meetings of the Emily Dickinson International Society. I have met so many people on these journeys and each one, in their own way, has helped shaped this book. I have learned from, and been inspired by, them — and, of course, Emily. To those who I have written about here, I give my most sincere thanks. And I wish to give thanks for the many more people who touched my life during my journeys whose stories I keep secret — at least in this book.

I extend special thanks to David Porter, professor emeritus at the University of Massachusetts, for his continuous encouragement, Daniel

Lombardo for his tremendous assistance and friendship, to Sara Gaunt for her help in editing, and to Gian Lombardo for making this book a reality. I am grateful to Tevis Kimball and Kate Boyle, who kept a "reserved" space for me at the Jones Library. Susan Raymond and Julie Howland at the English Department at Amherst College were also a great help. I owe my experiences in Amherst to the Ministry of Education in Japan, the American Council of Learned Scholars, and the Fulbright Scholars Program. Many thanks go to my generous colleagues at Mie University and at Osaka Shoin Women's University who allowed me time off to pursue these studies. I also gratefully acknowledge the support of Osaka Shoin Women's University, which made the publication of this book possible. Finally, I would like to thank my parents and my sister, Makiko, for their love, and Kissa, a stray cat who sustained me during difficult times.

I include, and excerpt, many of Emily's poems and letters throughout the text. Emily's poems were published posthumously in variety of collections put together by Thomas Higginson (Emily's mentor), Mabel Todd, Millicent Todd Bingham (Mabel's daughter), Martha Dickinson Bianchi (Emily's niece) and Alfred Hampson (Martha's collaborator). In all of these publications, Emily's words suffered alterations at the hands of these editors who smoothed out her irregular rhymes and rhythms, adjusting them to suit the tastes of the period. Finally, in 1955, a complete three-volume set of unaltered poems was published by Thomas H. Johnson, which has been regarded as the standard text. Johnson counted 1,775 poems and basically arranged them chronologically. Poems in this book are identified by their Johnson numbers (for example, J1755).

Johnson also edited *The Letters of Emily Dickinson* in 1958, aided by Theodora Ward. This collection included 1,049 of Dickinson's letters as well as some of her prose. These letters are arranged chronologically and given a number that begins with "L." Letters in this book are identified by their Johnson edition numbers (for example, L10).

(In 1998, *The Poems of Emily Dickinson*, a three-volume set edited by Ralph Franklin was published. Since this new text has a different numbering system, many books and articles that refer to Emily's poems often use both numbers [for example, J1755/Fr1779]. In this book, however, only the Johnson numbers are used to in order to avoid confusion.)

# Introduction

WHILE STUDYING EMILY DICKINSON IN THE UNITED STATES, I HAD a chance to meet another Japanese scholar who was also here to do research. He remarked, "If you write a book about your experiences here, it will reveal not what you did, but rather that you did nothing at all." This book will certainly reveal that I did not spend all my days single-mindedly devoted to research. Studying Dickinson was not the only reason for my extended stays. I didn't want to write a scholarly work about her, but a book that might also be enjoyed by people who don't usually read poetry. I hoped to write about Dickinson, the poet I love so much. I hoped readers would get to know something about her life, read some of her best works, and even get glimpses of recent information and controversies about this elusive poet.

When some people hear the word *poetry*, they turn away from it, thinking perhaps that it's too esoteric. But *words*, the tool poets use, are what we use in our daily lives. Poets are simply professionals and how they use words is what grips us. Poets give us the gift of conveying what we let pass unnoticed, or what we have noticed but do not know how to express. I would like to see poetry more widely embraced and accepted in people's daily lives. That said, few poets are more appropriate for this than Emily.

Of course, Dickinson can be dealt with purely as an object of study, but I tend to regard her as someone who lives in me. I cherish my days in Amherst, where it was possible for a twentieth-century Japanese woman to get to know a nineteenth-century New England poet. I was also forced to ruminate about my native country and the meaning of living abroad as a Japanese woman. This book also addresses the issue of language, since my daily life was spent speaking English, I read Dickinson in English, and much of my career has been devoted to translating her into Japanese.

One person told me that attempting to encompass all of this would be too much to do in one book, advising me to choose just a single focus. But these things were so closely knitted together that it is almost impossible to separate them. Another person encouraged me to follow my own way. However, I have to admit, I did not think I wanted to write so much about myself when I set to work. American-type individualism is generally considered a negative trait for the Japanese and other Asians. Yet, I cannot talk about Emily without also talking about myself. And even though my English and my manner of building a story are sometimes faulty, I feel my experiences are worth recording since this struggle to express myself is, in many ways, universal.

Emily's poems can make you feel as if you are speaking with a kindred spirit. As a result, a reader might be more inclined to open his or her mind. You can read her poems not just objectively but by drawing her into yourself. I rarely talk about myself with others quite so much, but when I discover someone who shares an interest in her, I find myself revealing what is within.

What also sparked my interest in Emily was my attraction to her lifestyle. I was drawn to her shyness and reclusiveness. And yet, ironically, I came abroad to study her, traveling widely and meeting new people in the course of my Dickinson studies — hardly the life of a recluse. This book is about two cultures coming together, about an introverted Japanese woman who chose to live more as an extrovert through Emily.

There is always something about Emily that excites me. There is always someone who I will meet and get to know through her. I came to Amherst for the first time simply because it was *her* town. So every incident that befell me and every person that I met was through her. Without Emily I would not have made these journeys. If I never embarked in search of her, I would not have found so much.

*For all those who love Emily Dickinson
and all those who have helped make
Amherst my second hometown*

# Discovering Emily

I BEGAN TO LEARN ENGLISH IN JUNIOR HIGH SCHOOL AND, IN GENERAL, MY peers and I found it interesting and we liked the subject. However, in most cases, including mine, this fascination did not last long. I simply could not remember the spelling of all those words. I could manage in the beginning, but after a few months, it was hopeless.

Pronunciation was also a problem. Why is the *ti* in *tiger* not pronounced the same as the *ti* in *Tim*? And at the end of the word *tiger*, why is the *r* not pronounced with a *ra, ri, ru, re,* or *ro* sound? I found the rules incomprehensible and the explanations unconvincing. And in the beginning, with my limited vocabulary, everything looked so inconsistent. That is, after all, one of the distinguishing characteristics of the English language — its irregularities.

I scored only twelve points out of twenty on one of the vocabulary tests during the first term I studied English. It was such a great shock that I resolved to make every effort to memorize words. Only then did the structure of a new sentence like "Who is that lady?" — which we were to learn at the beginning of the second semester — become clear to me. And so I narrowly escaped hating English.

English became my favorite subject during my second term, when in English Club — one of the after school activities — our adviser wrote this untitled poem by Christina Rossetti on the blackboard:

> Who has seen the wind?
> Neither I nor you:
> But when the leaves hang trembling,
> The wind is passing through.
>
> Who has seen the wind?
> Neither you nor I:
> But when the trees bow down their heads,
> The wind is passing by.

She explained that the second and fourth lines of each stanza have the same ending sounds and that this was done by the poet on purpose. Rhyming was new to me since rhymes are seldom found in Japanese poetry. I was fascinated with the new beauty of rhyming sounds. For a non-native speaker of English, switching the *I* with the *you* (from the second line) in order to create the rhyme of *I* and *by* in the next stanza came as a staggering revelation to a young Japanese girl.

While I am grateful that our English teacher was astute at teaching grammar, he spoke with a very pronounced accent even in Japanese, so I cannot possibly say if his English pronunciation was good — even to be polite. The young female teacher who taught some other English classes, and who also advised the English Club, spoke beautiful English and her students' pronunciation was far better than ours. I was envious.

With my newfound knowledge of rhyme, I listened to her read the poem sweetly, and I marveled about what a melodious language English is. The sentimental message of Rossetti's verse appealed to my adolescent heart, and I savored the charm of the poem.

For homework, the teacher told us to memorize the poem so that we could recite it in front of others. Having never done anything of the kind before, we were all surprised by her request. On top of my amazement I was mortified. I murmured the poem to myself, asleep and awake. As a result, even now, many years later, I can recall and recite Rossetti's lines effortlessly.

I realized in hindsight that this exercise was a very good practice for developing our skills in English pronunciation and rhythm. I tried to reproduce the beauty of the sounds I sensed as much as possible. And now, whenever I teach English poetry I make it a rule to ask my students to memorize and recite a poem or two. Many students might resent it, but some are challenged to attempt a very long poem, which delights me. Nothing could be better to help students of English develop a sense not only of poetry but also English itself. To recite a poem in a foreign language in front of people can be embarrassing for some. I would prefer not do it, but out of fairness I force myself to recite a poem for them. With this self-imposed obligation and given my own pleasure, I have gotten into the habit of reciting poems while taking a walk or soaking in a bath tub.

Yaso Saijo (1892–1970), a famous Japanese poet, translated that Rossetti poem into Japanese. Although it was a good translation, I didn't like its halting manner. It lacked the naturalness and elegance of the original. When you read a poem written in its original form and language, it soaks into your body and soul, even when it might be difficult for you to understand its content completely — a gift only an intimate knowledge of the poem's mother tongue can bestow. Naturally, I loved the beauty of Japanese poetry, but with this exposure to Rossetti's poem I came into contact with a new beauty.

I found a collection of Christina Rossetti's poems at the school library and read it. For the most part, I just enjoyed the illustrations and glanced at the words or looked for rhymes. I still had a very poor command of English, having studied it for less than a year. And I looked for other collections of relatively simple poems in English for junior high school students, but I had a hard time finding them.

Fortunately, I did discover two ways of deepening my understanding of both poetry and the English language. The first was a monthly poetry column in a woman's magazine called *Fujin-Gaho (Ladies' Journal)* to which my mother subscribed. For each issue, the poet Jun Takami (1907–65) chose one foreign poem, translated it, and presented it with an illustration that he felt reflected the poem's content. Each year, he chose a theme such as "My Favorite Woman Poets" or "My Favorite Love Poetry" and all of the monthly translations conformed to his chosen theme. Takami's column was very popular and lasted for several years. My mother had saved back issues, and it gave me great pleasure to clip out his column. I cut out every one and made a special anthology of my own, which I still treasure.

It was in the course of my reading this column that I encountered Emily Dickinson's poetry for the first time. I found a sketch by Chagall of two women drawn with simple strokes along with the following poem:

> To make a prairie it takes a clover and one bee,
> One clover, and a bee,
> And revery.
> The revery alone will do,
> If bees are few.   (J1755)

I remember specifically the feeling Dickinson conveyed of the wind sweeping over a spacious prairie. Takami explained to the Japanese audience that a prairie is not a meadow, but is peculiar to the United States and is very spacious broad grassland. At that time, I did not think much about the fact that Dickinson had never traveled to the Midwest and had never seen a true prairie so I missed the play of revery and imagination. However, Dickinson's imaginative power was strong enough for a girl who lived far away from a prairie to be swept by the wind that could be imagined blowing across it — strong enough for a girl whom the word *prairie* could have been just a technical term learned in a geometry class.

Takami also noted another Dickinson poem that had appeared in a previous column. I was intrigued and desperately wanted to read the other poem, but that particular issue was missing from my collection.

The second channel I had for discovering English poetry was a bimonthly magazine called *Junior Soleil*. It was published for dreamy romantic girls and I began to subscribe to it when I entered senior high school. The magazine was founded and edited by Jun'ichi Nakahara (1913–58), who captured the hearts of Japanese teenage girls. In post-war Japan, his magazine provided beautiful fantasies in contrast with a poor and drab daily life, thus giving the minds of many Japanese women opportunity to run free.

Along with fashion, etiquette, and stories, *Junior Soleil* had a page of English poetry and pretty illustrations. I encountered some Dickinson poems in *Junior Soleil*, including:

> A word is dead
> When it is said,
> Some say.
> I say it just

>           Begins to live
>           That day.   (J1212)

I thought that this poem really spoke the truth: it was brought to me across time and space — rendering them insignificant. It was surprising to me that a simple truth could be conveyed through such simple words that could be understood by someone just beginning to learn English.

When I left for college, I discarded all of the articles I clipped from *Junior Soleil* except for the poetry pages because it didn't feel appropriate to hold onto such fantasies when I was embarking on the serious adventure of learning. Later, when I was recording notes for the meeting of an English literature society, I discovered that the name of one of the professors was the same as of that of the editor of the *Junior Soleil* poetry page. A friend (who was also a *Junior Soleil* fan) and I timidly approached him and asked him about it. A bit embarrassed at the sight of two women with girlish enthusiasm in their eyes, he confessed that it was a side job when he was a graduate student at Tokyo University. He had not saved any of his contributions to the magazine. I made photocopies of my collection of clippings for him.

To this day, I still appreciate some of his translations. For example, "I say" on the fourth line expresses Dickinson's assertion or belief. A direct Japanese translation of that "I say" into Japanese as either *watashi-wa iu* or *watashi-wa iitai* would be weak since in the former the ending sounds feeble because the *i* and the *u* elide and in the latter the ending *iitai* has too many sounds. His translation as *watashi-wa iou* was both strong and concise since the *i* and the *ou* are pronounced separately, giving the air (aurally) of the power of determination. I have continued to take cues from his translations. This professor later became president of an English literature society in Japan. And so, one could argue that *Junior Soleil* had quite an effect on our culture. For example, its existence helped solidify my, as well as my friend's, life-long dedication to poetry in English.

It was during my time as a university student that the first anthology of Dickinson's selected poems translated into Japanese was published. During my forty-five minute train commute from my home in Osaka to my university in Kyoto, I would be totally absorbed in the anthology. I thought, "this is *my* poet." Emily Dickinson simply became "Emily" to me. With each poem I read I found myself pleasantly surprised to find that she expressed exactly what I was thinking. It was then that I stopped scribbling my own poetry.

I had started writing poetry as a junior high school student. My writing was a kind of short prose poetry that originated not from any strong impulse to write but was simply a kind of a diary entry. Emily had written all that I wanted to express. For me, it was futile to make my own poor attempts at poetry when Emily's poems contained all of what I wanted to say — and more. I made up my mind then and there to read her all my life, although I was not yet serious about studying her. Now, when I am introduced as a Dickinson scholar who has translated her works into Japanese, I am often asked if I write poetry myself. My answer is that after discovering Emily, I stopped writing poems, which, although it may sound strange, is the truth.

I completed the general education curriculum for the first two years at the university, and had to choose an elective. I was a student in the Department of Literature but I was still uncertain about my major. At that time, the fields of anthropology and comparative literature were not yet developed and there were almost no such courses at my university. In addition, I was afraid and began to feel ashamed that I knew so little about Japan and my own culture. I decided to major in Japanese literature. For my senior thesis, I chose to study *haiku*.

When it was time for me to graduate, I found I wasn't ready to give up my student status. After graduating with a degree in Japanese literature, I declared an American literature major with the intention of studying Imagism because I was particularly interested in the fact that the American Imagists had been influenced by haiku. But as I studied the Imagists I found that beyond that influence, as poets, the similarities were not that deep and I did not find them very interesting. I had avoided Emily, but after this long hiatus I came back to her.

I purposely avoided studying Emily academically; I feared my love for her poetry would prevent me from thinking of her dispassionately as an object of study. I was not accustomed to the idea of "studying" her poetry: I relished it too much. To read her poems translated into Japanese was easier, but I wanted to read them in her original language, especially those poems that had not yet been touched by a Japanese translator's hand. A friend in the United States sent me the Modern Library's Dickinson collection. Finding the time to carefully read the book poem by poem was not easy. So somewhat selfishly, with this aim in mind, I chose Emily as the theme for my second thesis. I am still studying her today.

I began my teaching career as a member of the faculty at Mie University in 1972. Soon after that, I found a newspaper announcement for "a poetry reading on a street corner." It was an outdoor performance in the plaza of the Maru Building in downtown Osaka, where businessmen passed by, hurrying on their way home in the twilight. The performers read *Heike Monogatari*, a Japanese classic, and several other modern poems. In Japan, at every New Year at the royal court, *tanka* (5-7-5-7-7 syllable poems) are recited in the presence of the royal family. However, in our daily lives, we no longer get together to recite tanka. For the Japanese, a certain awkward embarrassment comes from hearing modern poems recited out loud. Since we are no longer accustomed to it, it sounds too artificial. This was another reason for my fascination with English poetry: it is far closer to everyday English and colloquial language than Japanese poetry is to everyday Japanese. I was thrilled to learn that live poetry readings were emerging in Japan. This particular amateur troupe recited each poem from memory and I enjoyed their performance.

I had been translating Emily's poems into Japanese, but without rhyme being natural to the Japanese language, the original sound and rhythm schemes were lost in the translation. It was almost impossible to retain the poems' original aural qualities. I did my best to retain or re-create at least some of the melodiousness when I translated the poems into Japanese. I made it a rule to read my translations aloud as often as I could. It occurred to me that I could ask the poetry troupe to read my translations during one of their rehearsals. In that way, I could hear what I felt would be a more objective reading by listening and noting whether my Japanese had a natural flow. Their reading also gave me the added benefit of listening to performers who had greater talent than my own.

So I decided to contact the leader of the troupe even though I did not have any pretext for an introduction. My enthusiasm possibly made it easier for her to ignore this breach of protocol, and she immediately suggested that the troupe perform my translations publicly. We worked together to put several poems into groups under the titles of "Prologue," "I Am Emily Dickinson," "Emily & Nature," "Love of Flame," and "Wandering Soul." At the beginning of each grouping, we added a brief explanation, which also was read. Thus the basis for the script "In Praise of Emily Dickinson" was born. The troupe's performance exceeded my expectations; I was totally astounded. I invited them to come to my university for another performance. I thought a classroom would do, but I decided to rent a space at the Culture Hall, which could hold a larger audience. The performance was announced not only to students but also to local residents. I was filled with anxiety about covering the costs for publicity and hall rental. And, of course, many believed that no one would attend. But to my great relief and joy, the house was almost full. As the father of one of my students, a retired newspaper reporter who had helped publicize the event, said, "There is nothing as fearless as an amateur."

At the performance, the readers recited my translations from memory. My translations have changed a lot since then, and I felt a bit anxious listening to the troupe reciting them, wondering if my words were even worth memorizing. Yet, I never listen to the recording of the performance without feeling encouraged, even when I am exhausted or crest-fallen.

The performance consisted of not only Dickinson poems, but also the work of one modern poet and a novelette by one of the greatest nineteenth-century Japanese writers. After the successful performance, I began to think about planning a program on a much smaller scale — a poetry reading of just Dickinson poems. Emily is well known among the literary set in Japan, but not among the general public. I began to think that this might be my opportunity to introduce and popularize the poet. I began to work on answering this new calling.

The first purely Dickinson poetry reading took place in a small, private museum. The Ariake Museum is nestled among the trees of Nagano prefecture in Matsumoto, in the scenic highlands in the heart of Japan. The fabulous location was far more than we expected. We thought our poetry reading series would start in some small, office-like space, but we ended up at a small but tasteful and elegant museum hidden in a beautiful forest. A friend of mine, an artist, designed a gorgeous playbill. Given that this was our first performance, things did not go entirely smoothly. Yet afterwards, I was surprised to receive a letter from a total stranger who was in the audience; she wrote, "I was bored with my daily life as a housewife, but when I heard Emily Dickinson's poems that day, it was like an icy sword thrust into my heart." That encouraged me to continue.

Although the poetry readings required a lot of work and preparation — negotiating to rent a hall, setting up for the performance, identifying the audience, advertising in the local media — the satisfaction I felt was great. From 1985 through 1989, we gave ten performances — at coffee shops, galleries, colleges, and elsewhere. During this brief period, we did more as an amateur troupe than I had ever imagined.

Not long afterward, in 1989, an acquaintance suggested I give a series of lectures. In my efforts to popularize Dickinson and as a teacher with many years of experience, the idea for a small lecture series had certainly occurred

# Amherst, 1986

I WAS SITTING ON THE PLANE ON THE RUNWAY AND ITS ENGINE BEGAN TO roar. Even though it was too late to turn back I asked myself whether I should be going to Amherst. I quickly affirmed that I should — that I had to. When my dream of living abroad at last came true, the location could not be anywhere but Amherst. Everything I had been up to that point laid the basis for that decision and it had taken forty years to come to that decision. I was teaching at Mie University, and one person from my department was chosen to study abroad through the Ministry of Education every year. There were many candidates, but I was fortunate enough to be selected to travel to the United States in 1986. I stepped off that plane in Boston that August and headed straight to Amherst, Massachusetts, where I would be a visiting professor at the University of Massachusetts, delighted to be studying Emily Dickinson in her home town.

Amherst was named for Lord Jeffery Amherst of England, whose portrait hangs at the Mead Museum at Amherst College. During the American colonial period, the English forces, under his leadership, defeated the French at

## In Search of Emily

Louisbourg in Canada. To commemorate the victory, many new towns in America were named after him. When Amherst, originally a part of the neighboring town of Hadley, was established in 1759 the town took his name. Later in his career, General Amherst distributed blankets infected with smallpox in a conscious effort to kill Native Americans. In the 1970s, there was a movement to change the name of the town, but somehow the name remains. In the 1980s, the last direct descendant of Lord Amherst died in England.

The locals pronounce it as *AM-erst*, with the accent on the first syllable and not on the second as one would assume having some knowledge of American English. Whenever I buy a bus ticket from Boston now, I pronounce the town as *Am-HERST* (accent on the second syllable) to avoid being asked to repeat myself (just another peculiarity of English — all those variations of pronunciation). In a country dominated by cars, there is no direct train service from Boston to Amherst, so one has to endure a three-hour bus ride. The alternative is to fly into Bradley Airport near Springfield, Massachusetts, and continue for another hour by bus or car.

Summers in Amherst are not stiflingly hot, but winters are freezing cold, with an average daily mean in January of 24°F and 72°F in July. Dickinson praised summer as the best season in many of her poems. Still, many of the locals now escape north to Vermont or southeast to Cape Cod for weekends in the summer. In the fall, the changing leaves are stunningly gorgeous. Indian summer is warm and bright, but, as time goes on, there are more cool and foggy days. The winter I experienced was an ordinary one, and not especially cold. Of course, there were days when it snowed long and hard, and it was best to hole up in a warm room and wait until the town plows had cleared the snow from the streets. By contrast, I found most residents were not well prepared for the heat of summer. When it was unusually hot, it was almost unbearable for them. Most of the houses were only equipped with electric fans, and even then there weren't enough of them for every room.

On the day after my arrival in Amherst, I was pleasantly surprised to find that the laundry I had done the night before was already dry. New Englanders seem to take rainy days in stride, whereas in humid Japan, once you get wet, it takes some time to get dry and get comfortable again. This might explain why there's a wide variety of umbrellas in Japan as compared to the few choices in Amherst.

The Connecticut River runs through the states of Connecticut, Massachusetts, Vermont, and New Hampshire. The river carved out the Pioneer Valley where Amherst is located. The Holyoke Range — a series of small mountains — border the town on the south and Pelham Hill borders on the east. The locals have somewhat sarcastically nicknamed the area the "Happy Valley" because some residents have tried to make sure no one is offended by anything or anyone — that everyone should live together happily (a worthy goal, but an impossible task). A short distance from the center of town, I discovered a landscape where cows graze peacefully in wide pastures, and decided that, regardless of its connotations or recent history, "Happy Valley" was an apt name for the area. When the Japanese think of the United States, many of us tend to think of big cities and skyscrapers, yet much of the country consists of small towns in vast natural settings.

The two chief towns of the Happy Valley are Amherst and Northampton, and the valley's cultural nexus is its five colleges — Amherst College, the University of Massachusetts, Hampshire College, Smith College and Mount Holyoke College. The town of Amherst covers is 28.7 square miles and supports a population that grows during the school year to around 35,000, of which the University of Massachusetts at Amherst accounts for over 25,000 of those residents (its students). Amherst seems to sleep during school holidays and summer break, awakening a bit grouchily whenever the students (and their accompanying noise) return. In many respects, it is a typical American college town. It is also a town that is very aware of its history and of its "celebrities." And, of course, Emily Dickinson is one of Amherst's most celebrated personages. For example, in 1986, the film version of Isak Dinesen's *Out of Africa*, starring Meryl Streep and Robert Redford was popular. In a local newspaper, I found a cartoon titled "Out of Amherst" with Thoreau holding Dickinson in his arms.

Amherst College, established in 1821, is one of the oldest private colleges in the United States. Emily's grandfather was one of its founders, and both her father and brother were treasurers of the college. As a result, the institution is deeply connected with her. Its academic standards are high and the personal guidance of its 1,500 students is well-organized. As a result, the college always ranks high in national surveys of satisfaction among faculty and students. The school's library and other buildings surround a quadrangle of well-manicured lawn and trees, which commands a scenic view of the Holyoke Range. There has been a long history between Amherst College and Japan. While I was in Amherst, a Japanese television station broadcast a documentary program on the life of Joseph Neesima (1841–90), a Japanese student and a class of 1870 Amherst College graduate. In 1871, Neesima returned to Japan and started a small English school that eventually developed into Doshisha University.

Doshisha has enjoyed a close relationship with its founder's alma mater, sponsoring an exchange program of professors and students. At Amherst College, a portrait of Neesima is hung along with other distinguished American graduates in Johnson Chapel. The portrait carries the words, "Presented by His Classmates," and a plate is attached that reads "A dwelling place / For the light of friendship / Crossing the sea" written both in English and Japanese, presented by the Amherst House of Doshisha to Amherst College. According to a professor from Doshisha University whose time at Amherst coincided with mine, even during the fiercest fighting between the United States and Japan in World War II, the portrait was not removed. As I listened to this professor talk with pride, I realized that this long history of friendship is really a treasure.

The University of Massachusetts at Amherst, or UMass, was founded as a small state agricultural college in 1863 at the same time that a state technical college (now the Massachusetts Institute of Technology) was established in Boston. The first president of UMass was William S. Clark, who incidentally helped found Sapporo Agricultural College, now Hokkaido University, in Japan in 1876. Although he stayed in Japan for only a year, he had a great influence among Japanese students. He is best remembered for his farewell words to his students, "Boys, be ambitious!" — words that every Japanese school child knows to this day. Oddly, in Amherst he is barely remembered. It wasn't until 1991 that a memorial commemorating the centennial of Clark's death was erected; it sits on a high ridge at the eastern gateway to the campus, the location of a home once occupied by Prof. and Mrs. Clark and their children. UMass is now the largest public university in New England. The campus is huge; it would take half a day to walk around its borders. The library, a tall tower, along with campus's skyscrapers appear suddenly in the peaceful rural scene when you drive into town.

Hampshire College was established in 1970 and emphasizes innovation and independent inquiry by its students. Mount Holyoke College in South Hadley is the oldest college for women in the nation. The forerunner of this college was Mount Holyoke Female Seminary, which Emily attended as a student. Smith College in Northampton has also produced many distinguished women. Both Mount Holyoke and Smith are about a half-hour's ride from Amherst.

Open cross-registration enables students to take courses at any of the institutions. This unique and progressive system has admirable cooperative aspects: multi-campus academic and cultural programs, expanded course offerings, access to all of the libraries' collections from any campus, and much more. Collaboration among the five institutions helps to maintain facilities and equipment that would be beyond the financial reaches of any single school. This, in fact, is one of the big attractions the five-college cooperative offers to high school students thinking about their higher education.

The five-college cooperative was incorporated in 1965. It is easy to surmise that a lot of work and preparation went into coordinating the five administrations. Clearly, it was worthwhile and it now seems quite successful in spite of the problems that inevitably accompany it.

Among these five colleges there is a fare-free bus system that links the campuses during the school term. The transit bus system is indispensable, and it offers good side jobs for UMass students as drivers. When a bus approaches town, it stops first at Amherst Common, where students often play ball games or lie on the green with books in their hands. Some of the buildings around the common are the dormitories of Amherst College, but there is also the Lord Jeffery Inn. Popularly referred to as the Lord Jeff, it is an elegant hotel founded by Amherst College alumni. When one of the princes of Monaco was a student at Amherst College, Princess Grace stayed at the Lord Jeff. Other lodgings in Amherst include unique bed-and-breakfasts, and a clean and functional campus hotel at UMass that was built to train hotel management students. Yet, the Lord Jeff might be the only place in this small town graceful enough for a princess.

Next to the Lord Jeff is Grace Episcopal Church, in front of which grew a big *katsura* tree, called "Giant Tree," which Dr. Clark brought from Japan. The town hall with its clock tower is located next to the church. The steeple of a white church is the tallest building in the town center — it and the town common comprise a typical New England scene.

I visited Amherst's different churches on Sundays, hoping to get a sense of the religious atmosphere in the area and to understand that context of Emily's sensibilities. Though she did not subscribe to or attend any particular church, it can safely be said that spirituality permeates most of her work. I could easily imagine the imposing religious influence of one hundred years ago. During her lifetime, revivals were often held that attempted to bring back that burning fervor of the founding Puritanical period of the country. Despite being surrounded by all this religious zeal, she decided against attending church. The implications of this resolution were clearer to me after I gained a better idea of the religious atmosphere of the area. Emily's individualistic spirituality was so important to her that she even risked being ostracized by the community for not following what others did and by refusing to attend church.

Jonathan Edwards was one of the best known Puritan ministers and the church where he preached is in neighboring Northampton. My visit there further illuminated for me the religious climate of the region. American history cannot do without Edwards and Puritanism or Calvinism, his austere preaching of the "angry" God — the absolutely categorical choice of eternal salvation or damnation. Although Edwards was active roughly a century before Emily's time, it cannot be denied that the proximity of his religious mission left a legacy that continued to affect the religious atmosphere of Amherst when she was alive.

One sunny afternoon, when I attempted to enjoy a sandwich and a beer on the Amherst Common, I learned that in some New England towns, the "Dry Law" — that one cannot buy, and sometimes not even serve, alcoholic beverages — still prevails. It is so different from Japan, and illustrative of New England's historical Puritanical spirit.

Like any good academic town, Amherst has a good number of bookstores. Not long after I arrived, I decided to spend an entire day touring them. For a book lover, this is the best way to get to know a town. I drew up my itinerary and left the L.A.O.S. Religious Book Center, affiliated with Grace Church, for last because it seemed the least accessible. The store, which sold not only religious books, music, and cards, also had a children's book corner where I found a copy of *Winnie-the-Pooh* in Latin.

I had discovered Pooh as a little girl in Japan when my mother bought a new edition for my sister and me when we were very young. Once I began to learn English, I sought out the original, and had the added pleasure of comparing it with the Japanese translation. For example, I was bowled over by an issue of layout in the original. An illustration in the book shows Pooh climbing a difficult tree, with the accompanying text:

> He
> climbed
> and
> he
> climbed
> and
> he
> climbed

*Amherst, 1986*

Since most Japanese books are printed to be read from top to bottom, this wit is lost in the Japanese translation.

I had a smattering of Latin at my university and was thrilled to find this childhood favorite in Latin and excited at the prospect of having these new pictures — namely, Pooh in a toga and Pooh and Piglet in Roman armor.

After a long day of visiting bookstores, I decided to treat myself to tea at a small delicatessen called the Black Sheep. I was impressed that even a small rural town like Amherst could give birth to a chic shop like this one. Just several months after it opened in 1986, the Black Sheep was voted the best of the valley in a local newspaper.

There I found lapsang souchong tea, which I had long been wanting to try, but which was sold only in large quantities in Japan. I had to travel all the way to Amherst to find it sold in tea bags and to finally have a taste. I also found crystallized violets. Each lovely transparent bag had a white ribbon that complemented the violet sugar. And each bag had an individual price tag affixed to it, which I found somewhat charming. As I sipped my tea and admired my purchases, I remembered that in Emily's room in the Dickinson Homestead there was violet embroidery on the cradle blanket she had used as a baby. It had proven an afternoon of discoveries and reflection.

From then on, I would make little purchases in town and share them with the French Canadian woman, Christine, from whom I was renting a room. She began to look forward to my showing her the trifling treasures that I brought back from town, saying, "I have bought something 'foolish' again." In addition to the Pooh book, the crystallized violets, and the tea, there were beautifully and carefully made poetry books for children, as well as kaleidoscopes and more.

And that is how I fell in love with Amherst.

# Emily's Amherst

IT WASN'T LONG, OF COURSE, BEFORE I BEGAN TO EXPLORE AMHERST MORE directly for its connections to Emily. The first place to visit is the Dickinson Homestead. At the northwestern corner of Amherst Common is an intersection. From there, you walk east along Main Street. In less than ten minutes, there's a grand red-brick building behind the trees on the left-hand side. This house is The Homestead — referred to as "the Mansion" by locals. The impression of grandness is stronger when looking up from the portico, with its Greek-style white columns ascending from the stone stairs. Old prints and photos of the house indicate it used to be at street level, but when streetcar construction began, Main Street was regraded, leaving the house higher.

The Mansion was built by Emily's grandfather in 1813. She was born in 1830 in this house, but it was sold three years later to help relieve some of her grandfather Samuel Fowler Dickinson's severe financial difficulties. The family then lived in a house on nearby North Pleasant Street until Emily was twenty-four-years old, when the family returned to the Mansion. The house on North Pleasant has, unfortunately, been replaced by a service station. It must have been a matter of pride and satisfaction for Emily's father, Edward, to re-establish possession of the home his father had built. Emily spent the rest of her life there until she died at age fifty-five. The house has been owned by Amherst College since 1965. Guided tours of the house are given several days a week. I cherish the way in which touring the house brought me closer to Emily.

Upon entering, there is a hallway with a staircase to the second floor. To the left of the hallway are two parlors with several portraits hanging on the walls. One of the portraits is a replica of the painting of Emily (at nine years old), her brother, Austin, and her sister, Lavinia. (The original work hangs at Harvard University.) Painted by an itinerant portrait artist, who used a mannered technique, the three children look indistinguishable and it is not easy to decipher the facial characteristics of young Emily.

In the parlor, I am always struck by a feeling of solemnity due to the historical significance of the room. In 1862, Emily wrote a letter to a Mr. Higginson, a critic whose lead article in *Atlantic Monthly* had caught her eye. Even though he was a total stranger, a relationship bloomed and their correspondence lasted until her death. Eight years after Emily sent her initial letter, Higginson called on her for the first time. He sent a letter to his wife later that day about his impressions:

> A large county lawyer's house, brown brick, with great trees & a garden — I sent up my card. A parlor dark & cool & stiffish, a few books & engravings & an open piano — Malbone & O D [Out Door] Papers among other books. A step like a pattering child's in entry & in glided a little plain woman with two smooth bands of reddish hair & a face a little like Belle Dove's; not plainer — with no good feature — in a very plain & exquisitely clean white pique & a blue net worsted shawl. She came to me with two day lilies which she put in a sort of childlike way into my hand & said "These are my introduction" in a soft frightened breathless childlike voice — & added under her breath "Forgive me if I am frightened; I never see strangers & hardly know what I say —" (L342a)

*Malbone* and *Out Door Papers* are both Higginson's works. Belle Dove is possibly an acquaintance of Mr. and Mrs. Higginson. The moments described in Higginson's scribbled note transpired in the parlor and each time I visit it, I replay their meeting in my mind. Emily presents us with a mystery here:

## In Search of Emily

What do the day lilies represent? In Amherst, these flowers are abundant during summer time. This suggests to me that she was saying, "I am as commonplace as day lilies." Maybe she meant "I am Amherst" since day lilies could be considered representative of the town. On one occasion, Emily signed herself as "Amherst" at the end of a letter. Day lilies are named as such, it is said, because their blooms last only a day (although they can last far longer). Perhaps her message was "I am fleeting yet intense." Another Dickinson scholar finds meaning in the literary language of the day lily: coquetry.

On the second floor, Emily's room is in the southwest corner of the house. It has plenty of natural light, with windows on both the south and west; the south side faces Main Street, the busiest street of the period. Today, overgrown trees obstruct the view below, but in Emily's time she could observe clearly what was happening on the bustling thoroughfare — it was "the world."

The pieces of furniture in the room are reproductions of the time and what would have likely to have been in her family's possession: a Franklin stove, a sleigh bed, a small table and chair (originals now at Harvard University), a bureau, and so forth. Hanging from one of the windows is a basket on a string, placed there according to an episode recorded in a memoir of one Emily's friends: Emily made gingerbread and lowered it in the basket to the children down below. Fond of children, she knew very well what they liked.

On the floor is a *tatami* mat, of great interest to Japanese visitors, for many Japanese houses still have tatami-matted rooms. What is here is more precisely called a *goza*, just a thin surface of tatami matting. During Emily's time, there was a great interest in all things Oriental. Americans imported porcelain from China. When the articles were shipped, they were wrapped with this matting to protect them from breakage. Americans soon found that the mats could make rooms more comfortable: a warm carpet that covered the floor in winter would be rolled up and replaced with a tatami mat in summer. Their use became quite fashionable in nineteenth-century New England.

Whenever I visit Emily's room and see the mat, I recall one of her poems, which is often regarded as her answer as to why she chose to live a secluded life:

> The Soul selects her own Society —
> Then — shuts the Door —
> To her divine Majority —
> Present no more —

> Unmoved — she notes the Chariots — pausing
> At her low Gate —
> Unmoved — an Emperor be kneeling
> Upon her Mat —
>
> I've known her — from an ample nation —
> Choose One —
> Then — close the Valves of her attention —
> Like Stone —     (J303)

    The soul has selected her friends, so wonderful and divine that she rejects other suitors, be it a winner of some game pompously riding in an extravagant carriage (or it could be also interpreted as a victor of a battle) or an emperor, the noblest and most powerful on earth. This scene is intriguing — a maiden turning a cold shoulder. Yet she is not arrogant since she mentions her domain as a *"low* gate," noting that she is poor. Since she has found an invaluable person who meets her requirements, the worldly high standards no longer matter. The Chosen One is described as "society" (line 1) and "majority" (line 3), which induces a reader to think that the soul has found many, or at least some number of, friends. In fact, as the third line from the end indicates, only one is chosen. Then, who (or what) is the "only one"? Taking the suitor image literally, it could be a lover. But a metaphorical reading allows that it could be regarded as her "Muse," — that is, "Poetry" — or as "God," or as "the soul," itself. According to these interpretations, Emily's life as a recluse was filled with talking to herself — that is, writing poetry or communing with God. At the end of the poem, *elastic* "Valves" are compared to *solid* "Stone." Emily's careful presentation of details moves readers to read all of her works carefully. The ending of the poem with "like Stone" sounds so serious and solemn that it almost rejects others' intervention. This "Stone" could be an allusion to "gravestone."

    I first read this poem decades ago as a student in Japan. My professor told us of his visit to the Dickinson Homestead and of the tatami matting in her room. He suggested, as one interpretation, the visual image of an emperor kneeling on a tatami mat. He did not stick with that reading though and for the first time I saw how an insight into a writer's life might lead to a particular interpretation. It widened the possibility of appreciation.

    Of course, we have to consider that the mat in the poem is not necessarily the one spread in the room; it could have been a door mat. That even an emperor could not be allowed to enter into the soul's room expresses her determined attitude.

Professor David Porter at UMass was my sponsor and advisor during my stay. He taught classes, advised the tour guides at The Homestead, and even worked as a tour guide himself on occasion. The only time we were free to meet with each other was the hour between guided tours. We chatted while sitting on chairs in Emily's room. It gave me a thrill to be able to spend time, however brief it might be, in this way, in the space where she had *lived*.

On display in the room is one of Emily's white dresses. It has a pocket, which was not common at the time. She might have put pen and paper in that pocket so she could jot things down as they came to her. Since she confined herself to her room, and since her sister Lavinia was almost the same size, Lavinia stood in for Emily when a dressmaker took measurements. Emily's white dress has been sentimentalized as a bridal dress, a symbol of her unrequited love for a man, whom some think had a wife and children. Looking at that dress in that room, however, the theory seems implausible because the design and material of the dress are distinctly non-bridal. Another theory, that her skin was too sensitive for dyes, seems more likely. For many years, the white dress was in the closet of Emily's room. At the international Dickinson conference in Washington, D.C., in 1986 it was displayed on a mannequin, on which it came back to Amherst. It was then exhibited in a glass case for more than ten years. The dress and the mannequin indicate that she seemed to have been rather small. In a letter, she referred to herself as "jumbo Emily" as a joke. And although we know that she was small, her exact size cannot be determined.

The garden on the east side of The Homestead remains spacious, and in Emily's time the lot also included a meadow across the street. What she wrote in one letter — "I do not cross my Father's ground to any House or town" (L330) — can be interpreted as follows: She was not confined to just her room, but rather to fourteen acres in which she could take walks.

In one corner of the yard are flower beds, where one can enjoy beautiful flowers each season, especially in summer, although the layout is not an entirely faithful restoration of Emily's garden. Examples of her herbariums show her horticultural and scientific zeal; in fact, there used to be a conservatory attached to the main building in which she spent days tending and observing flowers and trees.

She communed not only with her flora and fauna, but also with "Nature's People" (from J986), among them birds and squirrels. In Japan, squirrels are rare in built-up areas. So when I came to the garden at The Homestead for the first time, I was so thrilled to find a squirrel that I imagined it was a descendant of the many squirrels in Emily's poems:

> I'll tell you how the Sun rose —
> A Ribbon at a time —
> The Steeples swam in Amethyst —
> The news, like Squirrels, ran —
> The Hills untied their Bonnets —
> The Bobolinks — begun —
> Then I said softly to myself —
> "That must have been the Sun"!
> But how he set — I know not —
> There seemed a purple stile
> That little Yellow boys and girls
> Were climbing all the while —
> Till when they reached the other side,
> A Dominie in Gray —
> Put gently up the evening Bars —
> And led the flock away —     (J318)

Her expression "The news, like Squirrels, ran —" is so unique, and the image was not completely clear to me until I came to Amherst and saw the squirrels bouncing by with tails as big as their bodies, drawing quick, continuous double half-circles.

Emily spent her adolescent years in the house at North Pleasant Street, behind which is the vast expanse of West Cemetery. The proximity of the house to the cemetery is supposed to have influenced her meditations on death and her numerous poems on the subject. When I visited the site of the North Pleasant Street house and the graveyard, I immediately sensed the influence they must have had on a young girl like Emily. The years she spent in this house were her most impressionable, and outside the Civil War was taking the lives of thousands of young soldiers. Emily must have seen a funeral nearly every week. (Her own gravesite is in this cemetery.)

She attended Amherst Academy from the ages of nine to sixteen. The building no longer exists: a memorial stone erected downtown on Amity Street, opposite the Jones Library marks the spot. The academy, opened under the leadership of Dickinson's grandfather, and Noah Webster, eventually helped spawn Amherst College. The school provided an excellent education — especially in the sciences — and set the highest standards of the time. This education had a strong influence on Emily: Professor Edward Hitchcock's writings focused on the importance of seeing the glory of God in the mysteries of nature. The scientific underpinnings of her poems were awakened at this time.

After graduating from the academy, she attended Mount Holyoke Female Seminary, now Mount Holyoke College, for about a year, from 1847 to 1848. The seminary was founded by Mary Lyon, a woman with a burning sense of religious mission. At first Emily was happy there, but she soon experienced pressure with regard to the religious issues. Those who could not accept Jesus were called "No-hopers"; she chose to be a "No-hoper" until the end. Although some scholars and historians have asserted, rather dramatically, that she was the only student at the seminary who resisted Jesus, there were, in fact, others. Nevertheless, it is certain that Emily suffered at the seminary as she tried to come to terms with her faith and the orthodox religious atmosphere of the time. She sent a letter to Abiah Root, a friend and former classmate at the Amherst Academy:

> When I am most happy there is a sting in every enjoyment. I find no rose without a thorn. There is an aching void in my heart which I am convinced the world never can fill. I am far from being thoughtless upon the subject of religion. I continually hear Christ saying to me Daughter give me thine religion. . . . I am continually putting off becoming a Christian. Evil voices lisp in my ear — There is yet time enough. I feel that every day I live I sin more and more in closing my ear to the offers of mercy which are presented to me freely —   (L10)

Emily's father sensed the difficulty of her situation, and her poor health, and decided about half-way through her first year not to send her back for another. She wrote to Root three months before she was to leave the seminary for good:

> I have neglected the *one thing needful* when all were obtaining it, . . . you may be surprised to hear me speak as I do, knowing that I express no interest in the all-important subject, but I am not happy, and I regret that last term, when that golden opportunity was mine, that I did not give up and become a Christian.   (L23)

Mount Holyoke is a thirty-minute bus ride from Amherst; and although it must have taken much longer by carriage in Emily's day, it is not far away. Yet, she was homesick.

Without a specialized education or one particularly focused on literature, she had to polish her literary and linguistic abilities by herself. In a letter to Higginson she wrote: "I went to school — but in your manner of the phrase — had no education" (L261). Later in the same letter to Higginson she mentions that "for several years, my Lexicon — was my only companion —." This lexicon was the 1844 version compiled by Noah Webster. Surely, she pored over it. Yet her love for the Webster dictionary was special, since Noah Webster was the very person who worked with her grandfather in founding the academy and Amherst College. His statue can be found on the Amherst College campus.

Emily and Helen Hunt Jackson were classmates at Amherst Academy. However, their personalities were too different for them to find a good friend in the other. Yet Jackson emerged in her forties as the acclaimed poet and writer, "H.H." Her writings included *Ramona* and *Mercy Philbrick's Choice*, as well as other writings on social issues. She became acquainted with Emily's work through Higginson, and Jackson so passionately encouraged her to publish that Emily, somewhat embarrassed, shrank back from her advances. Although it is uncertain just how much she appreciated Emily's true value, Jackson was the only contemporary writer who thought so highly of her; she wrote to Emily, "You are a great poet." (L444a).

Jackson's house in Amherst is about ten-minute walk, or half-mile, south from the town center. It is painted ochre with green shutters in the fashion of the period and those bright colors serve to remind me of the contrast between Jackson's happy personality and Emily's more somber one. After a meeting between the two women, Jackson sent a letter that clearly depicts the differences between the two women:

> I feel as if I had been very impertinent that day in speaking to you as I did, — accusing you of living away from the sun light — and telling you that you looked ill, ... but really you looked so white ... I felt like a great ox talking to a white moth, and begging it to come and eat grass with me to see if it could not turn itself into beef!   (L476a)

Jackson's determination to publish one of Emily's poems was so strong that when she wrote Emily a letter asking permission to publish it, Jackson was already in the process of having it printed in a volume titled *A Masque of Poets* (1st edition, 1878). A number of alterations were introduced into the text, teaching Emily a bitter lesson of what it meant to have her work published.

> Success is counted sweetest
> By those who ne'er succeed.
> To comprehend a nectar
> Requires sorest need.
>
> Not one of all the purple Host
> Who took the Flag today
> Can tell the definition
> So clear of Victory
>
> As he defeated — dying —
> On whose forbidden ear
> The distant strains of triumph
> Burst agonized and clear!    (J67)

In the revised, printed version "the" was inserted before "sorest" (line 4), line 8 became "So plain, of Victory," and line 12 became "Break, agonizing clear." In addition to some other punctuation and capitalization changes, the printed version had no stanza breaks. Emily's poem was printed anonymously (as were a number of other poems) for the pleasure of readers to conjecture authorship. The publisher thanked Emily for her contribution and reported to her that some readers thought Ralph Waldo Emerson was its author. As flattering as it might be to be compared to a great writer, it did not move her. The editorial alterations show how little and also how great the differences are.

It is interesting and ironic that Emily's first poem printed in book form and altered without permission is on "success." However, the poem's main concern with agony, particularly mental agony, is apropos.

The entire Dickinson family was intimately involved in the affairs of Amherst. Austin Dickinson, Emily's brother, played an important part in the construction of the First Congregational Church, and Amherst Common was landscaped and beautified for the community under his direction.

On the opposite side of Main Street, not far from The Homestead stands a railroad station. It appears somewhat forlorn, as it serves mainly freight trains and offers only a midnight service for passengers to New York or Canada. From there, they are not popular destinations. However, the station was once a thriving center. Edward Dickinson, Emily's father, was one of the most enthusiastic railroad supporters. He was, in fact, a director of the society whose mission it was to bring the railroad to the town in the 1850s when railroad-building fever was at its height. The Amherst-Belchertown Railroad built the line, and the first train went from Palmer (a town 20 miles to the southeast) to Amherst on May 9, 1853. A week later, Emily wrote to her brother Austin, then a student at Harvard:

> While I write, the whistle is playing, and the cars just coming in. It gives us all new life, every time it plays. How you will love to hear it, when you come home again! (L123)

In another letter, Emily told him about New London Day, when more than 300 people from New London, Connecticut, paid an official visit to Amherst through the invitation of the railroad company. Emily's reclusive attitude makes a vivid contrast with the turmoil of activity:

> The New London Day passed off grandly — ... Father was as usual, Chief Marshal of the day, and went marching around the town with New London at his heels like some old Roman General, upon a Triumph Day.... I sat in Prof Tyler's woods and saw the train move off, and then ran home again for fear somebody would see me, or ask me how I did. (L127)

Emily left a few poems about trains that leave us to wonder whether she liked or loathed this symbol of modern technology. In the following riddle, "it" refers to the locomotive:

> I like to see it lap the Miles —
> And lick the Valleys up —
> And stop to feed itself at Tanks —
> And then — prodigious step
>
> Around a Pile of Mountains —
> And supercilious peer
> In Shanties — by the sides of Roads —
> And then a Quarry pare

> To fit it's Ribs
> And crawl between
> Complaining all the while
> In horrid — hooting stanza —
> Then chase itself down Hill —
>
> And neigh like Boanerges —
> Then — punctual as a Star
> Stop — docile and omnipotent
> At it's own stable door —   (J585)

Here the train is described using the familiar image of the iron horse; the train coming into a tunnel is described as "paring a quarry." Jesus nicknamed James and John the "Boanerges," meaning "sons of thunder" (Mark 3:17). Whenever I heard the whistle of the train at night in Amherst, it no longer sounded proudly and loudly "like Boanerges" but rather it was a lonely sound that encompassed the history of the train industry, its proud past and present neglect.

Just east of The Homestead is a large, elegant Italian villa-style house now owned by the Amherst Women's Club. It was once the house of Leonard M. Hills, who ran a successful straw hat manufacturing business and became president of the Amherst-Belchertown Railroad, for which Emily's father was a promoter. The Hills family and Emily exchanged flowers, Christmas remembrances, and letters. About forty of Emily's letters to the Hills survived, including one of condolence when the Hills lost an infant child.

In back of Emily's brother Austin's house, a stately manse sits on a small hill overlooking the town. Now called Marsh House, it is owned by Amherst College. The house was originally built and owned by Luke Sweetser, the first president of the Amherst-Belchertown Railroad. Emily often wrote to the wife of Luke's only son, John Howard.

Behind the Amherst town library stands the Strong House, which is now in the possession of the Amherst Historical Society. It is open to the public and tours that include talks on the building and its period furniture are available. Among the items on display is a cradle used by Helen Hunt Jackson as a baby. There are also many possessions that belonged to Mabel Loomis Todd — the first president of the Amherst Historical Society — including clothes, pictures, paintings, and things she brought back from trips (including to Japan) she made with her husband David Todd.

Todd and her husband lived on Spring Street, one block south of Main Street, close to The Homestead. Austin Dickinson cut a new road through the meadow south of his house; the Todds then bought the land from him, and built their house. The Todd's house, called the Dell, remains a good example of the Queen Anne style, although the colors of the house have changed. At the east end of Spring Street, two stone posts erected by Austin marking the property can still be seen.

Mabel came to Amherst with David, who became the director of the observatory, and professor of astronomy and navigation at Amherst College. They came to know the Dickinson family. Eventually, with David's consent some way or other, Mabel and Emily's brother Austin began to have a romantic relationship, which lasted for fourteen years until Austin's death. Since he was a leading figure in town, contributing much to the community, their relationship was a kind of public secret, without open censure. A book of literary criticism, *Austin and Mabel* was published in 1984, revealing their love letters.

While knowledge about this affair is integral to any Dickinson study, people pay too much attention to it. It should be noted that Mabel came into Emily's life in the last two years of her life, after she had written most of her poems; there is little possibility that her love poems, for example, reflect their relationship. Mabel was so talented that once she painted a picture for Emily, for which Emily was happy enough to send a poem in return. At another occasion, Mabel sang at The Homestead for Emily, who listened from the floor above. While Mabel was eager to see her, Emily on her part would never meet Mabel. This experience induced Mabel to call Emily "a myth," which, for better or worse, contributed to making the stereotype of Emily Dickinson.

The most important facet of Emily-Mabel relationship is that Mabel was the first editor of her poems, along with Higginson. In editing their collections, they not only selected poems that would suit the sentimental tastes of their period but they also made many alterations to follow conventional prosody — something that Emily would have definitely abhorred. However, it must be admitted that Emily was too ahead of her time to be accepted at face value. Looking at the primitive typewriter Mabel used (in the possession of the Jones Library), one realizes that just to type manuscripts must have been a tough job. Without these efforts, Emily's poems would not have survived.

Southeast of the UMass campus, about ten-minute walk from downtown, is the Wildwood Cemetery. Austin Dickinson, his wife, Susan, and their three children are buried here. Austin's gravestone is a small one, inscribed only with his initials, A.W.D. Some say this was his wife's revenge for his long-term affair, but that remains unproven. By ignoring Austin's infidelity, Susan has suffered unfair characterizations. But more recently, greater emphasis has been placed on Susan's role as Emily's literary confidante. One of the more extreme theories even maintains there was a lesbian relationship between the two women. Near the gravestones is a memorial stone dedicated to Austin from the townspeople. Mabel and her husband are also buried in this cemetery, with flat, black gravestones with flowery designs and astronomical symbols, respectively.

In Amherst, these buildings create a living history, making Emily's time come alive. And in this town in 1986, the 100th anniversary of her death, I remember attending a play at UMass where I was introduced to an old lady, who was the widow of UMass Professor Frank Prentice Rand, for whom the theater was named. I had heard that Mrs. Rand liked Emily Dickinson very much, and made it a rule to attend the cemetery walk held every year on the anniversary of her death. At that time she was ninety-six years old, making her born the year Emily died. And as I held Mrs. Rand's hand in mine, I felt Emily's existence draw closer to me. This contact made me feel that Emily is still very much alive.

# An American Education

During my first year-long stay in Amherst, I audited several courses that had something, directly or indirectly, to do with Emily Dickinson. I did so in the hopes of gaining a better understanding of her. It helped me also to get a glimpse of the inner workings of an American college education.

As the beginning of the new school year neared in September, I paid a visit to the UMass Textbook Annex. I was astonished to find a gymnasium filled with row upon row of steel bookshelves. I was pleased to find books there that I could seldom find at ordinary bookstores, and other books useful to my teaching in Japan. After this experience, I never visited another American college or university without spending hours checking almost every shelf in its bookstore.

I noticed that American professors are cognizant of bestsellers and other popular contemporary works. These books are always assigned as textbooks across the curriculum. It struck me as a good idea to attract students' attention to the other different academic disciplines through contemporary hot topics, encouraging students to see that education can have a direct impact on their future.

As I flipped through the used textbooks, however, I saw how easily this kind of dream can be broken. It is rather sad to note the point in the texts when the markings disappear, to see how many students lost interest along their way, assigned too much to read, too much to write. In some cases, I found that the marginalia were so off the mark that it was no surprise that the student floundered. Other times, I'd come across a note and think "right on, good job" when the underlined parts were on target and perceptive.

To a Japanese scholar, the amount of required reading in the United States is quite astounding. In Japan, professors usually assign undergraduates to read one book a year per course. They feel that is reasonable since they expect students to read more on their own. Yet, in American literature courses, the Norton anthologies are as thick as dictionaries. Skimming the shelves at the Textbook Annex, I discovered a course for which the list of required books included Erich Maria Remarque's *All Quiet on the Western Front*, Shohei Ohoka's (1909–88) *Fires in the Plains* (a Japanese novel), and Penguin's anthology of *First World War Poetry*. I was impressed that this course on war literature incorporated such a wide variety of works — Eastern and Western, poetry and prose.

During my textbook search, I discovered that a professor was assigning *Poems of Emily Dickinson* for her course. I was surprised to find that she, too, was a visiting professor — from France. I decided to audit her class. Our shared status as visiting professors taught me an important lesson. Until I met her, I was embarrassed or even irritated by questions like, "Why do Japanese people like Dickinson? Is it because her poetry is so much like *haiku*? What aspects of Dickinson especially appeal to the Japanese?" The questions were innocent enough but I couldn't help but think, "I read Dickinson because I like her work. I am not necessarily representative of all Japanese readers. I really don't know how the larger Japanese population regards Dickinson." And yet, when I met the visiting French professor, similar questions started pouring from my lips: "What aspects of Dickinson especially appeal to French people? How do the French regard her and how often do they read her poems?" I realized few Americans have the chance to meet foreign Dickinson scholars. When they have the chance, it is quite natural that they should ask those kinds of questions. This experience with the French scholar taught me the importance of explaining Japanese attitudes toward Dickinson to other cultures. And in fact, I had always been interested in how my culture affects my reading of her work. Since then, I have consciously and deliberately taken up that issue in my scholarship.

As luck would have it, the French professor's landlady was Jean Mudge, who once lived at The Homestead as its resident curator. She was the author of *Emily Dickinson and the Image of Home*, and in collaboration with other tour guides, she had also published a booklet, *Emily Dickinson: Profile of the Poet as Cook*. It was a delightful book with recipes from Emily and Susan Dickinson; I had long hoped to translate it. I took advantage of meeting Mudge and obtained her permission to translate the recipes. Another Dickinson scholar and I collaborated on the translation and it was published in Japan as *Emily Dickinson no Oryori Techo (Emily Dickinson's Cookbook)* in 1990 with the addition of colorful pictures of the dishes.

Meeting Mudge gave me a chance to ask another long-standing question. One of the recipes Emily left behind is for a black cake, a variant of fruit cake. In the spring of 1883, Emily's next door neighbor, Mrs. Sweetser, sent her a gift of some flower bulbs. Emily sent a thank-you note, accompanied by a bouquet of flowers grown from the bulbs themselves, together with the following recipe:

> Black Cake –
> 2 pounds Flour –
> 2 Sugar –
> 2 Butter –
> 19 Eggs –
> 5 pounds Raisins –
> 1 Currants –
> 1 Citron –
> pint Brandy –
> — Molasses —
> 2 Nutmegs –
> 5 teaspoons
> Cloves – Mace – Cinnamon –
> 3 teaspoons Soda –
> Beat Butter and Sugar together –
> Add Eggs without beating – and beat the mixture again –
> Bake 2 or three hours, in Cake pans, or 5 to 6 hours in Milk pan, if full –   (L835a)

I was surprised at the quantities: two pounds of butter and nineteen eggs! But it would have been for a great many people, such as family members and guests at Christmas time. And it would last for days, even weeks.

Once the ingredients are collected, you simply have to beat them together. Fortunately, modern conveniences make the preparation much easier. I occasionally make this cake, which tastes, to me, like New England a century ago. Rich and sticky, it is meant to be enjoyed in small quantities. With currants, raisins and molasses, the cake is black as can be.

In Japan, currants and molasses can be found in foreign food markets. Citron is a different story. I did not even know what it was and once substituted lemon rind. Mudge told me that I could get citron in almost any American supermarket: the small jelly-like red, green, and yellow cubes, are sold in round plastic containers. In Amherst, I bought citron and for the first time baked an authentic black cake.

Another course I audited was a graduate-level course on Puritan Literature. I was attracted by the course description, which included a field trip to Deerfield, Massachusetts. Part of Deerfield is a preserved (to the eighteenth century) historical section called Old Deerfield. I thought that this course might provide a chance to experience the religious atmosphere that dominated New England right up until Emily's time. A class visit to an Old Deerfield church would show how piously, and sometimes uncomfortably, parishioners were seated in their pews as the preacher sermonized from pulpit on high about an angry God.

The course also examined the works of Edward Taylor, a seventeenth-century religious poet. I was surprised to learn that Taylor was "discovered" by the Dickinson scholar Thomas Johnson. His name is a familiar one among Dickinsonians. Johnson made a major contribution to scholarship in the field when he edited a complete volume of her poems and letters. (As noted in the preface, I follow Johnson's notation for Emily's poems and letters throughout this book.) Taylor had been forgotten when Johnson found his works almost by chance among the curios being sold at an antique show. Taylor is among the first American poets, but he might have remained unknown without Johnson's discovery. (I was also surprised to find out that the teacher of this course had studied with Johnson when he was a student.)

While I was in Amherst I had the privilege to access the area's five-college system, wherein students and faculty of any of the five colleges — Amherst College, Hampshire College, UMass, Mt. Holyoke College and Smith College — can make use of the other participating colleges. I took the opportunity then to audit a course on Whitman and Dickinson at Mount Holyoke College, which was taught by Christopher Benfey, the author of *Emily Dickinson and the Problem of Others*. His book was a well-argued, philosophical one rather than the usual literary study of Dickinson. The same year I audited his course, he published another Dickinson book, *Emily Dickinson: Lives of a Poet*, a handy critical biography with illustrations and around thirty poems. Benfey's second book included pictures seldom seen in other Dickinson books and a poem on The Homestead by Jay Leyda, who is the author of a magnificent record of Emily's life titled *The Years and Hours of Emily Dickinson*, to which every Dickinson scholar owes a great deal.

Benfey's unique approach to Dickinson permeated the syllabus: Whitman and Dickinson were neatly compared — for example, how they each respectively treated the Civil War in their works. He ended the course with a poem — "The Impossible Marriage" by Donald Hall, which relates the impossibility of any marriage between Whitman and Dickinson. I'd heard of the poem before, but I'd never read it. I discovered that it was the perfect ending to the course by the use of coupled pairs of opposite words to succinctly characterize each poet and to portray the futility, and irony, of them ever making a "match."

I also took a history course at Amherst College on the Transcendentalists. Our professor informed me of an event in Stowe, Vermont, to commemorate the centenary of Dickinson's death. He was invited to give a lecture. It was a program open to the general public and sponsored by the National Endowment for the Humanities (NEH). It included three days of lectures, group discussions, and the performance of a play titled *Emily*.

The area president of NEH began his opening address with Emily's "Success is counted sweetest" (J67), which he dedicated to "all the Boston Red Sox fans." The audience replied with laughter in the wake of the team's defeat in the recent World Series. Dr. Richard Sewall, the author of *The Life of Emily Dickinson*, an indispensable biography for any Dickinson student, also lectured at Stowe. I had heard him speak before and always appreciated his great passion and love for Emily Dickinson; his spirit was infectious and created much enthusiasm amongst the other participants.

These classes that I was able to take made my life in Amherst busy and enriched, and I value those experiences for the ways in which they brought me closer to Emily and gave me a sweet taste of an American education.

# Amherst's Poet-Philosopher

NOT LONG AFTER I MOVED TO AMHERST, MY LANDLADY SAID TO ME, "You know, the house in which we used to live is located just a bit to the north of here. Our neighbor was also a famous poet; his name is Robert... Well, what *is* his last name? Not Frost..." And that was the first time I heard about the town's then-current resident poet, Robert Francis.

Francis was already eighty-five years old, and loved and respected by the people of Amherst. I read in the local paper that he was coming to the Jeffery Amherst Bookshop downtown to give autographs. The photos in the article showed a thin man with an elegant dignity about him, which made me think of a gracious crane. I was particularly taken by a snapshot of his smiling face. I couldn't go to his book signing, but I was free to attend a reading he was giving at a later date in Northampton, and I bought his latest book, *Travelling in Amherst*, for the half-hour bus ride.

Since the sun had not yet begun to set, I decided to walk from my rented room to the bus stop at UMass. I was familiar with a path through the dorms and the woods. With the slanting sunlight, I set out in the crisp early

October air. The horizon was already acquiring an orange tint, but higher up the sky was blue and bright, and a thin crescent moon was lightly hung. It was like a pastel work by Miró or a mobile by Calder. I stopped for a while to admire the colors and shapes in the grand composition in front of me. I took out my camera, searching for a good angle to capture the moment.

When I arrived at the concourse, the bus had just left. I could see it heading toward Northampton. I scolded myself, but all I could do was wait for the next bus, which was due in a half hour. I sat down on the ground and felt the cold from the surrounding air and the concrete. Traveling in Amherst myself, I submerged myself in Francis's book.

*Travelling in Amherst* is comprised of excerpts of the journal Francis kept from 1931 to 1954 (from age thirty to fifty-three). He was an extremely shy child, a characteristic that followed him into adulthood. He found it difficult to mix with others and after graduating from Harvard, he made up his mind to make a living at poetry, realizing that he hadn't the heart for more social or commercial pursuits. Early on, his poetry was not readily accepted by publishers, and he had to support himself until late in his life by playing the violin and giving lessons.

When Francis was thirty-two years old, his landlady introduced him to the poet Robert Frost. Frost, who was twenty-seven years older and already a great poet, encouraged him. Francis was influenced by Frost so much that he was occasionally criticized for poems that sounded too much like Frost's. It was a charge that hounded Francis for many years, but eventually, at the age of fifty, he wrote:

At last I seem to have recognized that, for better or for worse, I am a poet.

His published journal entries record his growth as a poet, a man, and an artist:

When a poem and I embrace, I have a peculiar impulse to pray, "Don't let me die, dear God, till this is over." The writing of poetry suddenly makes my life of high value to me.

Writing is not my sweetheart; it is my wife, it is part of me.

The poet is a spider, forever spinning. The novelist is a caterpillar, eating, eating great slices of life. But the poet spins his poetry out of himself, out of next to nothing.

> Writing poetry is like playing the harp: it often takes as long to get in tune as it does to play.

Francis's memoir includes humorous touches as well. A bachelor until his death, this passage reflects his dry, honest, and self-deprecating wit:

> This afternoon I heard someone coming up to my door whistling.
> It was a Fuller Brush man.
> "Is the lady of the house in?" he asked.
> "No," I said, "She is not in."
> "We don't often catch them in," he said. "But I want to leave her this little brush."
> "Oh, thank you," I said, taking the gift.
> "When would she probably be in?" he inquired.
> "That is hard to say," I answered truthfully.
> "Just like my wife," he said. "And here is a comb for you."
> He went whistling down the path.

Although not included in *Travelling in Amherst*, Francis wrote a poem as a dialogue between his mentor, Robert Frost, and Emily Dickinson. This dramatic poem is full of repartee between Frost and Dickinson. It starts in the middle of the night somewhere in downtown Amherst between The Homestead and the Lord Jeff. Frost recognizes Dickinson as "ghost while living / and haunting us ever since." They begin a poetic conversation, each in his and her own voice (with each poet often quoting the other), that tracks their common views until the points where they diverge. Dickinson is "called back" and Frost is "called ahead." But then towards the end of the poem, they both return to another commonality. Frost says to Dickinson, "We were both hiders. You / in your father's house. I / in the big buzzing world." And the poem ends on the struggle to believe. The poem also reflects Francis's retreat from the world and his sincere quest for true faith.

On the night of the reading, I arrived at the hall, and was relieved that it had not yet begun. Through the door, I saw the chairs arranged for the audience and I looked toward the stage and was startled to see an old man sitting there, very still. The spotlight was beaming on his face that portrayed a frightened look. His gaze seemed to be directed not toward something real, like the audience, but rather toward life itself. For a moment, I thought I was looking at a photo or a painting by a super-realist titled "An Old Man." This, I realized, was Robert Francis. It was already past the announced starting time, and a woman sitting in front of me began knitting. I could not take my eyes off this old man.

A few minutes later, the emcee gave a brief introduction and helped Francis make the few steps from his chair to the microphone in front. The reading began, and I found "a poet" there. His voice was small but firm. Each word was his. The verses that issued from his mind and body were his, and he recited them without glancing at any book or manuscript. He was, then, poetry itself on the wing of voice.

Poet Richard Wilbur once introduced Francis as "a New England poet with Japanese virtues." Wilbur said:

> What I meant by "Japanese" is this: in reading Francis, we seldom have a sense that a garrulous someone called "I" is standing between us and selected phenomena, telling us how he feels about them and what they signify.

Both Francis and haiku, with its plain but charged words, sing of nature and see life with a sincere and simple heart.

Although Francis's reading lasted only twenty minutes, instead of the usual hour, it was a full, solid time. And although many poets comment on each poem or talk about the context in which they wrote it. Francis simply said, "First, I'll read _____. Next, I'll read _____." When the audience applauded him at the end, he said, "While you sit, I stand. So, this is a standing ovation." We laughed and gave him a "real" standing ovation.

Francis stayed to sign copies of his poetry books, as well as his novels, and collections of essays, letters, and journals, which were spread out on a table before him. I approached to examine these various publications, and found people had already formed a queue. While he did his best to inscribe his name in a book with his trembling hand, some gave him warm words of praise, but he seemed too frail and tired to respond at length. When I got closer and could see more clearly what he was doing, I found that he only signed his initials, "RF." The "R" looked like a Chinese character (尺). Although I had never been very interested in collecting autographs, I suddenly realized that I wanted evidence in his own hand that I had come to hear him on this day. I held out my copy of *Travelling in Amherst*.

Seeing Francis made me wonder what it means to be a poet. Most poetry readings are organized by publishers in order to sell books (not just on that occasion but it is hoped in the future as well) and to stimulate people's interest in a particular poet, and moreover in poetry in general. Ideally, these readings promote culture, but the urgent issue for both publishers and poets is that they earn enough to eat. Whenever I read a newspaper or magazine article identifying someone as a poet, I wonder whether it is an appropriate appellation. I also wonder how the poet makes his/her living. In Japan, I once saw a woman at a station with a placard saying, "My husband is a poet. These are his works. Please buy some." It looked pathetic to me. I might have felt different if the poet had been standing there himself. I suppose he did not want to compromise, or did not want to beg. On the other hand, one of the most prosperous businessmen in Japan is a well-known poet and writer. Does poverty or wealth have anything to do with poetry? Somehow I find "selling poetry" more unscrupulous than "selling pictures," although both are nearly identical. Selling poetry seems slightly like selling your soul. It is a prejudice or misconception that I cannot shake. It is quite natural, then, that I am very much attracted to Emily's attitude as a poet. In one of her poems, she declares:

> Publication — is the Auction
> Of the Mind of Man —
> Poverty — be justifying
> For so foul a thing
>
> Possibly — but We — would rather
> From Our Garret go
> White — Unto the White Creator —
> Than invest — Our Snow —
>
> Thought belong to Him who gave it —
> Then — to Him Who bear
> Its Corporeal illustration — Sell
> The Royal Air —
>
> In the Parcel — Be the Merchant
> Of the Heavenly Grace —
> But reduce no Human Spirit
> To Disgrace of Price —    (J709)

The poem, abundant in references to money, is a declaration of refusing publication. Emily uses very severe words like *foul* and *Disgrace* with reference to publishing. In contrast, the purity of poor artists living in garrets is expressed with words like *White* and *Snow*, which are related to "the White Creator," God. In the last stanza, she criticizes the clergy by referring to them as the merchant[s] of the heavenly grace, but even they are better than those who publish!

It is surmised that Emily knew that her own poems were outstanding. She had ample opportunities to publish her work. If she had changed her style to suit the tastes of the period, she would have had even more chances. Yet she would never succumb to that pressure. She was always thankful for Higginson, her mentor, but she never followed his advice. Once she wrote to him:

> I smile when you suggest that I delay "to publish" — that being foreign to my thought, as Firmament to Fin —   (L265)

Out of her 1,775 poems, only ten were published in her lifetime, and that was not by her will but by that of her friends. If you choose the "profession of a poet," you cannot get away from selling your work, compromising with publishers, signing autographs, or holding poetry readings. Emily, with her rigidly purist attitudes, chose to simply be "a poet."

However, this purity needs support: It needs assurance that the poet can go on living without turning to selling the poetry. It also requires that, without a wide audience to write for, the poet will never fall into narrow self-contentment. Emily was lucky on both counts. Her father was well-to-do and she did not have to worry about her living expenses. Her sister-in-law, Susan, lived next door, and could offer her constructive criticism and remarks. Emily had many other friends, including celebrated people of the time, to correspond with and send poems to.

Without the emotional or material support that she had, but possessing the same tendency to evade society as Dickinson, Francis had to travel a long, tough road to fully realizing that he was a poet. Towards the end of his journal, in response to a Jones Library exhibit of a group of photographs of Amherst men taken many years ago, he wrote:

> Two of the portraits are labeled "poet," and I am one of the two. It gives me something of a start and also a satisfaction to be summed up in one word. I submit to the label. I am enough of a poet to be called a poet. Some day I may be more poet still.

He has continued, even until the age of eighty-five, to go on the road to be more *poet* still. He was both humble and sincere; he was as unpretentious as Emily was pure.

As I walked home that evening, I remembered the exquisite composition of the moon in the sky that I had seen earlier on my way to the reading. I looked for the moon and in the north, low on the horizon, I found seven beautiful stars, which took my breath away. Here in Amherst, the sky was vast and clear, making me forget life in the city.

Some time after I returned to Japan, my landlady sent me a letter, in which she added that, "By the way, it has been quite a while since Robert Francis passed away."

# Learning the Language

I FIRST CONTACTED THE KELTY FAMILY OF TRENTON, NEW JERSEY, WHEN I was a senior high school student in Japan. At that time, traveling abroad was not easy and studying abroad was just a fantasy for me. Diaries and letters written by Japanese who had studied abroad began to be published in book form. I devoured these books and they heavily influenced my life. One of these accounts gave me the idea of writing to newspapers in the United States indicating that I was looking for a host family to stay with. One of the two answers I received in response was from the Kelty family. The other response was from a girl who said that her family could not serve as a host family but that she hoped to be a friend. We have been pen pals for many years since; fortunately, she, and the Keltys, are honest people. However, when I reflect on what I did when I was young, I am simply dumbfounded at my recklessness of leaving my fate up to complete strangers.

After I received the response from Mrs. Kelty I confessed what I'd done to my parents. They were completely stunned. They objected to me going abroad since they felt that it would be difficult for me to both do that and prepare for college entrance exams. Everyone advised me to wait and to study abroad until I was a university student.

While I was attending university in Japan, I found that there were plenty of distractions and much to keep me busy that I became ambivalent about studying abroad — sometimes I was excited at the prospect; other times it would barely register with me. However, since I always had an interest in studying English, I enrolled in an intensive summer course in English; it was offered to any student attending one of the national universities and it was funded by several corporations. Discovering that there was money left in the budget at the end of the course, they offered a few students the trip of a lifetime — two months traveling in the United States from the East coast to the West with a two-week intensive course along the way in Michigan. It was an unexpected award. Finally, my desire to see the United States was going to be satisfied and I would get my first opportunity to meet the Kelty family. I managed to wrangle a few days free from the group tour schedule and the Kelty family took me to Trenton, where they lived. Living with the father, mother and two daughters (the elder of whom was almost my age) made me a little nervous, but having corresponded with them before turned the tide. And at our farewells, Lynne, the elder girl, and I hugged each other so tightly that the rest of the family was afraid we might suffocate the cat Lynne was also holding in her arms.

Since that initial trip, my desire to travel abroad has only gained in strength. I had traveled for brief periods or taken a summer course in Oxford, England, but I never had the chance to stay anywhere for an extended period of time. To travel and to live abroad are two different things. It is possible to travel abroad when you are too young to think about your future. However, for me, I realized that I needed a definite plan for the future so I could secure the necessary grants to travel. When, at last, I was granted a fellowship to conduct research on Dickinson in the States, I was already forty.

After my sister graduated from high school, she expressed her wish to attend college in Germany. Our parents, who now felt a bit of remorse over discouraging me, were supportive this time. In fairness, my sister's future profession was much clearer than mine had been; she went to train to be a concert pianist. She got married in Germany, has a job there, and has spent more years there than she has in her native country. I've learned much from her about living abroad.

During a chat with some of my students after a seminar I gave in Japan, I mentioned that my sister lived in Germany. One of the students exclaimed,

"How wonderful! It's such a dream to be able to live in a foreign country." I couldn't help but think her response naïve. In truth, I have found that living abroad is not so much a dream, but rather a source of conflict and struggle. As a foreigner, you must work hard just to be equal. Above all, you must constantly contend with an issue deeply rooted within yourself: your identity.

Once on a return trip to Japan, my sister was making her business arrangements when the Japanese gentleman she was talking to became suddenly indignant. I was with her at the time and we were both taken aback. We attributed it to the fact that my sister had uttered one businesslike sentence without any euphemisms. It was so subtle that we still weren't sure of exactly what had happened. We finally came to the following conclusion: my sister had talked to this older male as an equal, which was viewed as treatment unacceptable from young women in Japan. Life as a Japanese woman requires etiquette and deference — and a certain technique. My sister saw it as an interesting lesson: she could not act in Japan as she could in Germany. And yet, she added, "When I'm in Germany, I tend to be too demure; I am apt to draw back." It is a subtle complexity of her daily life and she must spend every day negotiating it in some way or another.

I deal less often with the subtle complexities of living abroad because I am generally there temporarily. However, at times, my situation as a scholar seems far more complicated than my sister's. The basis of literature is language, and when you are a non-native speaker of the language, you battle the language barrier all the time, and your situation can quickly seem hopeless. My American friends try to bolster my ego and compliment my English skills. The truth is, my grasp of English does not pose a problem for daily, run-of-the-mill interactions, but it is more of a challenge in my studies of American literature and, above all, poetry.

But there are times when I feel as though I'm being treated not as a human, but almost like an animal. When some people notice that you are a non-native speaker they treat you very kindly but they can also treat you as a child. If you cannot use difficult words or colloquial expressions, it is assumed that you are incapable of understanding the subtleties of the language. Finding it difficult to find words, you just mumble "Mmmmm, well . . ." It looks as if your brain itself does not function well. You are often regarded as less intelligent simply because you struggle with the language.

You also always have to be more vigilant and attentive, which is also very tiring. Professor Donald Keene, an American authority on Japanese literature, and a Japanese friend of his were talking in Japanese about literature when a dog barked somewhere in the distance. Because of the dog's howl, Keene missed one word that his Japanese friend had just uttered. Keene said, "Pardon?" His friend responded, "*Neigh* . . . an animal that neighs and runs clip-clop. Can't you see? *Neigh, neigh* . . ." Keene was dumbfounded but soon realized that the word he had missed was *horse* and that his friend had mistakenly assumed that Keene did not know the meaning of this word. Keene added: "Based on what we were saying and the level of our conversation, common sense should have told him that I must know the Japanese word for horse. If both parties were Japanese, they would easily come to a mutual understanding of the situation. When it comes to a foreigner, even the explanation itself descends to the level of an infant."

In another episode, Keene was hosting an educational television program on haiku. His guest was a modern haiku poet who said, "You understand Japanese literature rather well for a foreigner. But after all, you may not, since you like Basho (1664–1694) better than Issa (1763–1827)." I was surprised by the poet's impoliteness. This poet felt that a preference for Issa's subtle humor demonstrated sophisticated taste and if someone appreciated Issa then they could approach the true essence of Japanese literature. (But this was this particular poet's opinion; in my estimation Basho is a much greater poet.) Later in the show, when his guest had left, Keene made a point of saying that his preference of Basho to Issa was purely an issue of personal taste. In both cases, Keene was a perfect gentleman enduring the absurdity of the insult.

Keene is a leading Japanologist whose writings in Japanese often surpass what we Japanese write. In addition, the number of foreigners who study Japanese literature is still few, so his work is esteemed by the Japanese. Under these favorable circumstances, even a leading scholar had to experience the prejudices against non-native speakers. It's no surprise, then, that as a Japanese scholar of American literature and poetry, I occasionally feel helpless and incompetent.

When it comes to learning a foreign language, you definitely reach your limits, and you must struggle hard against them. Studying abroad when you are young improves your skills; my friends who were in the United States for a year during high school speak fairly good English. I envy them. Still, they will never be mistaken for native speakers.

A friend of mine in Japan, a former English teacher, lived in the United States for more than five years. Her two children were born and raised there, about which she told me a sad and funny story. She said, "I asked my son,

# Philadelphia and the Depth of Emily's Heart

For Dickinson scholars, Philadelphia has a special meaning. Emily seldom left Amherst, but at age twenty-four, she visited Philadelphia and heard Reverend Charles Wadsworth preach. Highly impressed, she began corresponding with him, referring to him as "My Philadelphia" (L750) in one of her letters. I could not miss the chance to see the city.

I began with a tour of Philadelphia and the first stages of American history: the Liberty Bell, Congress Hall, Old City Hall, among other sites. I visited the Graf House, where Jefferson composed a draft of the Declaration of Independence in a small room on the second floor. The ardent desires of the people who had emigrated from Europe to make a life in this new, hopeful country seemed to me to fill these huge buildings with a higher level of magnificence than their European equivalents. During the guided tours, the Americans seemed to hold their breath at the solemnity of the spots. Certainly, we all take liberty and equality for granted, but thinking about how much sacrifice and zeal had been necessary for these notions to be achieved and codified here proudly, I was touched along with the Americans on the tour. At first, the somewhat eclectic style of buildings created on such a grand scale looked awkward to me. I had the impression that the early Americans were trying to compensate for the absence of history and tradition with sheer size. In actuality, it is the perfect expression of the differences between old Europe and the new states; here in this young country Americans could start something afresh without being shackled by the baggage accumulated over centuries.

At Franklin Court, the restoration of Benjamin Franklin's house, not only the solemnity of history, but also the warmth of personality permeated the air. Franklin is well known even to the Japanese. I was assigned his *Autobiography* when I was a student. I was taken by his pragmatic and utilitarian attitude, coupled with his entertaining spirit. I enjoyed how Franklin could be so utilitarian even upon the most moralistic issues. After sending letters from the Franklin Post Office and lunching at Society Hill, I visited the Betsy Ross House.

I went back to the center of the town and the Arch Street Presbyterian Church, which Emily visited in 1855. I purposely made this visit my last one of the day. After gaining a sense of the city's history and atmosphere, I wanted to see what any Dickinson scholar should see. I suspected this might not be the original church, but it would have been a pity to go all that way without getting a glimpse of it.

The church, fairly large and imposing in the busy center of town, looked different from the photo I had seen in Dr. Sewall's *The Life of Emily Dickinson*. That church had several levels, each getting smaller as it rose heavenward. The modern church had just a domed roof on the main building. Returning to Amherst, I wrote a letter to Reverend Todd, the minister whose name I had found posted outside the church. I asked him about the relationship between the present church and the previous one. To my delight, I received a letter in response in which he wrote:

> The Arch Street Presbyterian Church which Emily saw was demolished in 1900. The present building was constructed in 1853–1855, not far from the Arch Street Presbyterian Church, and although Rev. Wadsworth was not a minister in this building, he was present at the first service. And some of his artifacts remain today.

He invited me to call on him during my next visit to Philadelphia. He seemed to have a lot to tell and I was sorry that I did not have enough the courage to knock on his door the first time.

Among the manuscripts preserved in the Rosenbach Museum and Library in Philadelphia were a few of Emily's. On that trip, which fell on a

*Philadelphia and the Depth of Emily's Heart*

Monday, the museum was closed so I decided to revisit Philadelphia a few months later. It would also give the opportunity to visit the Arch Street Church again and finally call upon Reverend Todd.

When I reached the church, I rang the doorbell. Reverend Todd answered and invited me inside. He was dressed somewhat formally and had a large build; he was rather old, but appeared strong and healthy. The room in which we made our formal introduction was something like an anteroom. On the walls hung pictures of the church's past ministers as well as the picture of the old church as shown in Dr. Sewall's book. The red velvet chair behind the big desk in the center of the room was brought from Charles Wadsworth's church in San Francisco, according to Reverend Todd. He gave me a tour of the meeting room and the main hall of the church. It was a fairly spacious church with a high ceiling and white Greek-style columns. It was truly majestic. Below the altar were other red velvet chairs, one of which was also from Wadsworth's church. Reverend Todd said, "Among the Dickinson scholars, I know Jay Leyda [author of the monumental *The Years and Hours of Emily Dickinson*, a daily chronicle of Emily's life] and Millicent Todd Bingham [Mabel's daughter] very well. In fact, I am a distant relative of the Todds. And I am also a distant relative of the Colemans, with whom Emily stayed when she came to Philadelphia. I am related to Emily Dickinson in many ways. And as the minister of this church, I am happy to say that I meet many individuals who are interested in or related to her."

I returned to the anteroom where Revered Todd pointed to a picture of a middle-aged man with a piercing glance and said, "Now, this is William." Reverend Todd had been a friend of Charles Wadsworth's son, William, and had officiated at his funeral. A picture of his father, Charles, showed a man wearing spectacles, which softened the appearance of his eyes. Because of this contrast of gaze I did not think William looked like his father.

After Charles Wadsworth died, Emily discovered that one of her father's acquaintances happened to be Charles' friend, James Clark. She corresponded with Clark for a while, and referred to William in several of her letters. In those letters, Emily mentioned only William and not Charles' elder two children. In one letter, Emily said she was like William. A subsequent letter clarified the resemblance as not a physical one but rather one of personality. Recognition of this resemblance made Emily happy and, unexpectedly, in recognizing Rev. Todd's connection to William, my heart leapt a bit, like Emily's must have.

It was surmised, partially by early scholars, that Charles Wadsworth was Emily's lover. They corresponded and, five years after their first encounter in

Philadelphia, Wadsworth visited her in Amherst. He visited again twenty years later. When he was sent from Philadelphia to San Francisco, it was a great shock to Emily. Although he eventually returned to Philadelphia in 1869, he still traveled all over the country to give sermons. Setting the lover issue aside, it is certain that he was an integral psychological guide for her, especially concerning religious matters. She called him "my dearest earthly friend" (L807), "a Man of Sorrow" (L776), and "a Dusk Gem, born of a troubled Waters" (L776), cherishing him as a fellow sufferer.

Unable to accept formal religion, Emily chose to follow the Transcendentalists' lead and commune directly with God through nature. She declared with humor and irony that even if you go to church regularly every Sunday, you can go to heaven only at the last moment — that is, at your death. But if you revel in nature, it gives you the feeling that you are already in heaven. She says, "the sermon is never long" (J324). Reverend Todd must have taken Emily's viewpoint to heart since the guideboard outside his church announced "A Series of Brief Sermons by Dr. Todd."

Of the 1,775 poems Emily left, nearly one tenth can be considered love poems. However, the exact number of love poems is debatable; in some of her work it is difficult to decipher a clear theme, while in others love is treated spiritually, and they might be better classified as religious poems. Still, it can safely be said that love is one of the strongest themes in her poetic range. In the poem that follows, love is depicted as being strong enough to penetrate a huge rock of the "universe," and yet despite its strength, love can be hindered. Some interpret this obstacle as love for a man who already has a wife, which is insinuated by the "Vail / unto the Lady's face."

> I had not minded — Walls —
> Were Universe — one Rock —
> And far I heard his silver Call
> The other side the Block —
>
> I'd tunnel — till my Groove
> Pushed sudden thro' to his —
> Then my face take her Recompense —
> The looking in his Eyes —
>
> But 'tis a single Hair —
> A filament — a law —

> A Cobweb — wove in Adamant —
> A Battlement — of Straw —
>
> A limit like the Vail
> Unto the Lady's face —
> But every Mesh — a Citadel —
> And Dragons — in the Crease —     (J398)

In addition to love poems, Emily left three love letters addressed simply to "Master." These letters were consequently known as the "Master letters." None of them were dated, but analysis indicated that they were written at different periods in her life. They were left in draft form marked with many corrections and it is not known if fair copies were made or eventually mailed to the intended recipient. These letters differ in their mood, but her spiritual anguish is evident in all three. Her passion is evident in the following excerpt:

> If you saw a bullet hit a Bird — and he told you he was'nt shot — you might weep at his courtesy, but you would certainly doubt his word. One drop more from the gash that stains your Daisy's bosom — then would you *believe*? (L233)

A bird hit by a bullet is supposed to represent Emily herself anguished by love, while the daisy also represents Emily, who devotes herself humbly to the beloved. This letter is an ardent confession of love.

In another one of her letters to Higginson, she declared, "My life has been too simple and stern to embarrass any" (L330). It is no exaggeration, since she seldom left her house and led a quiet life — ostensibly. But once her stormy inner life was revealed in the "Master letters," there has been much interest in to whom they might have been sent. Who inspired her to write so many love poems? It is no surprise that Emily, even posthumously, continues to hold her tongue. We certainly get a sense from her that the identity of her lover is not as important as the quality of her love: how deep and how ardent it is.

Dickinson scholars have identified several men with the potential to be Emily's "Master." One is Wadsworth and another is Samuel Bowles who took over his father's post as the editor of the *Springfield Republican*. Bowles was also a social reformer and, by the accounts of the day, a charming person. Emily exchanged letters with him, of one which goes:

> Dear Mr Bowles,
> I am much ashamed. I misbehaved tonight. I would like to sit in the dust. I fear I am your little friend no more, but Mrs Jim Crow. I am sorry I smiled at women... Good night, God will forgive me — Will you please to *try*?
> Emily

Bowles and his wife Mary were very good friends of the Dickinsons. When Bowles visited them, they must have disagreed while talking about the lives of women. The full letter is a rare, heartwarming example of a relationship Emily had someone in which she could so openly express her embarrassment.

There is an anecdote that testifies to their close relationship. On one of Bowles's visits to The Homestead, Emily declined to see him and he shouted upstairs: "Emily, you damned rascal! No more of this nonsense! I've traveled all the way from Springfield to see you. Come down at once." According to a cousin, Emily did come down. The exact relationship between them may not be known, yet it is unique for her to have had a friend who could have been so frank with her.

Both Bowles and Wadsworth were married, but in the later years of Emily's life a man entered whom she contemplated marrying — Otis Lord. Lord was well-respected as a Massachusetts Supreme Court judge and a member of the state legislature. He was a good friend of Emily's father and eighteen years her senior. After the death of his wife, Lord and Emily became very close and their relationship became intimate. In some of her letters to him, she unabashedly expresses her yearning for him:

> I confess that I love him — I rejoice that I love him — I thank the maker of Heaven and Earth — that gave him me to love — the exultation floods me. (L559)

> I kissed the little blank — you made it on the second page you may have forgotten — I will not wash my arm — the one you gave the scarf to — it is brown as an Almond — 'twill take your touch away — (L645)

Sadly, both families raised objections to the possibility of Lord and Emily marrying. The two of them might have also been hesitant about giving up the lives they had chosen. Before coming to a definite conclusion, Lord died, and was followed by Emily's death two years later. Emily's sister, Lavinia, who had served as a go-between for their correspondence, put two heliotropes in Emily's coffin "to take to Judge Lord."

*Philadelphia and the Depth of Emily's Heart*

Emily composed a love poem so fervent that when Higginson and Todd were compiling the first anthology of her poems, they hesitated to include it:

> Wild Nights — Wild Nights!
> Were I with thee
> Wild Nights should be
> Our luxury!
>
> Futile — the Winds —
> To a Heart in port —
> Done with the Compass —
> Done with the Chart!
>
> Rowing in Eden —
> Ah, the Sea!
> Might I but moor — Tonight —
> In Thee!   (J249)

The violent storm on the sea, which can also be interpreted as a landscape of mental images, and the fervent love synchronize: all the world seems to be swaying.

Though scrutinized for many years, it still remains impossible to give a definite answer as to whether Emily's lover was Wadsworth, Bowles, Lord, or someone else entirely. This mystery is truly Dickinsonian. What can be said of her with certainty is that she associated with people who were truly worthy of her, and her life, though generally perceived as lonely and spare, was in fact quite rich.

Having speculated about Emily's lover and afraid of taking up too much of the Reverend's time, I excused myself to leave. I asked him if I could, first, have a photo taken with him. He excused his appearance, "Because it was raining so hard, I wore these trousers; I am sorry they do not match the jacket." I was sorry, too; whenever I travel, I wear jeans that allow me to sit anywhere. And now, given the rain, they were stiff and tired looking. This man was such a gentleman that I wished I had visited dressed in my kimono.

I was a perfect stranger to him, but he greeted me warmly and acted graciously. I was grateful for the chance to meet such a noble person. Like Revered Todd, I am grateful for the ways in which my attachment to Emily has allowed me to transcend history and have unexpected encounters with many brilliant and kind contemporaries.

# Emily's Letters

THE COLLECTION OF EMILY'S LETTERS MAKE UP THREE VOLUMES (although a one-volume version is also available). The sheer quantity of these letters demonstrates the importance of correspondence to her, and now to scholars. Since she confined herself in later years to The Homestead, letters were the indispensable means of communicating with friends. She once wrote to Higginson:

> A Letter always feels to me like immortality because it is the mind alone without corporeal friend. (L330)

With the help of Theodora Ward, Thomas H. Johnson (who had also compiled *The Poems of Emily Dickinson*) published *The Letters of Emily Dickinson* in 1958. The collection included 1,049 Emily's letters and 124 prose fragments. Occasionally, letters from Emily's friend Helen Hunt Jackson, and Higginson's letters to his wife — recording his impressions of Dickinson — are also included. Per Emily's wishes, letters sent to her were burned by her sister, Lavinia. All of the letters in Johnson's collection are arranged chronologically and given a number that begins with "L." Since letters were such an integral part of her existence, Emily wrote several poems on the subject of letters:

> A Letter is a joy of Earth —
> It is denied the Gods —  (J1639)

---

> The Way I read a Letter's — this —
> 'Tis first — I lock the Door —
> And push it with my fingers — next —
> For transport it be sure —
>
> And then I go the furthest off
> To counteract a knock —
> Then draw my little Letter forth
> And slowly pick the lock —
>
> Then — glancing narrow, at the Wall —
> And narrow at the floor
> For firm Conviction of a Mouse
> Not exorcised before —
>
> Peruse how infinite I am
> To no one that You — know —
> And sigh for lack of Heaven — but not
> The Heaven God bestow —  (J636)

Emily's "letter to the world" is an appropriate prologue or epilogue for a Dickinson anthology:

> This is my letter to the World
> That never wrote to Me —
> The simple News that Nature told —
> With tender Majesty
>
> Her Message is committed
> To Hands I cannot see —

> For love of Her — Sweet — countrymen —
> Judge tenderly — of Me   (J441)

Emily often made her poems integral parts of her letters. In some cases, lines of prose from her letters are published in verse form, as in William H. Shurr's *New Dickinson Poems*. It is difficult to determine in her letters what is prose and what is poetry, clearly demonstrating the fine line and the intimate relationship between the two for her.

In Lewis Turco's *Emily Dickinson, Woman of Letters*, the individual lines in her letters were "selected, arranged, and augmented" into new poems and "centos." The result was largely the work of creation of the editor but is another illuminating way to uncover the poetry of her prose.

What might very well be Emily's last letter was addressed to her two Norcross cousins, Louise and Frances, whom she loved very much. They lost both their father and mother, the beloved Aunt Lavinia, when they were still young. Louise and Frances were twelve and seventeen years younger than Emily, respectively, and she seemed to have become a mother figure to them. When Emily went to live in Boston for a short time in 1864–1865 to have her eyes treated, the cousins traveled with her. The last letter sent to them included just two words, "Called back," and the date, May 1886. Emily died on May 15, 1886, and clearly she must have known that she was close to death. In the 1920s, Emily's niece Martha had "Called Back" carved on a new gravestone and placed at her aunt's gravesite in Amherst's West Cemetery.

In January 1885, the year before her last letter was sent, Emily wrote to her cousins that she had read a book titled *Called Back*, adding "it is a haunting story, and as loved Mr. Bowles used to say, 'greatly impressive to me.'" This novel, written by Frederick John Fargus, whose pen name was Hugh Conway, was very popular in its day.

When I first started my research on Emily at the Jones Library in Amherst, I found a copy of *Called Back* among the stacks. Richard Sewall, author of the great standard, *The Life of Emily Dickinson*, described it simply as a novel "in the sentimental-melodramatic mode at its worst." His comment whipped up my curiosity. Why would Emily be so impressed by a schmaltzy novel that she would refer to it on her deathbed? I decided to read it myself.

The narrator of *Called Back* begins with a brief description of a childhood condition that left him blind. (Perhaps this was part of the reason for Emily's interest; she suffered from a condition that threatened her eyesight and forced her, who otherwise seldom traveled, to go to Boston twice to see a doctor.) *Called Back* continues:

> One night, having a difficult time getting to sleep, I, Gilbert Vaughan got out of bed quietly. I had conceived the idea of groping around London. At first, hesitantly, but soon more and more boldly. I came across a house. And the key I had with me surprisingly fitted the keyhole of the house. Inside I heard a sweet female voice singing to an accompaniment played on a piano. Music being my special solace after the loss of sight, I approached the voice. There seemed to be several people, when the voice stopped suddenly and turned into a scream. And then, there was the sound of her tumbling off with a faint. I sensed that a murder had happened in front of her.
> 
> Unconscious of my blindness, I got out of the shade to rescue her and was I immediately caught. With the plea "I am blind. I have seen nothing," I was barely set free.
> 
> A few years passed. Having had an operation on my eyes and regained my eyesight, I went on a trip to Italy, where I met an exquisite beauty and was totally enamored of her. But, always close by her were a man with suspicious eyes on me and an attendant waiting on her. Even after coming back to London, I could not forget her. Realizing that I had fallen in love, I was obsessed with the idea of going back to Italy, when of all the places here in London I saw her and her maid. Having tried every means possible, I approached her. But the old servant coldly declared, "She is not for love or for marriage."
> 
> Out of my single-minded love, I got in touch with her uncle in Geneva, acquiring at last his assent to the marriage — with the conditions that I would not ask about her past and that all the living expenses would be on my shoulders as she had no dowry. The mysterious words of the maid, these conditions, and her consent given with no emotion — yet, love is blind, and the marriage in a rush was rather welcome for me. However, Pauline, the bride, was without memory of her past and without emotion, and almost like a doll!
> 
> I had to seek out the past. But her uncle was nowhere to be seen in all Geneva. At last that man with suspicious eyes was found, who introduced himself as Macari, Pauline's brother. Engaged in the political movement of Garibaldi, he talked about his activities during the meal using full gestures with a knife in his hand. Then Pauline, who was also at the table, uttered a

## In Search of Emily

scream, and fainted. She had remembered something in the past! She had been called back to the past!

Leaving Pauline fast asleep in care of the nurse, I started for faraway Russia. Macari had told me that the uncle was there now as a political prisoner. Would I find him in dark, misty Russia? . . .

What happened to me in Russia? After overwhelmingly complicated procedures and numerous mistakes, at last I had a chance to meet Alexander and got a special passport. Even after that there were many trials and errors, and in a dreadful prison in the far Siberia, among the people who looked like so many wriggling worms, I found the uncle eventually.

This was the past he talked of: Pauline and her brother were of mixed English and Italian parentage. Their parents died when they were still small children, leaving the administration of their property to their uncle, who spent the money for the political activities. Reached his majority, the brother had to be informed of the fact. The very interview had taken place on that London night. Macari was at the spot. He was no brother of Pauline, running persistently after Pauline who was now such a beauty, although she gave him the cold shoulder. On that night, Pauline, who knew nothing, was singing innocently at the piano. Macari, enraged with the contemptuous words of her brother, killed him with the knife he had with him. Seeing this tragedy right in front of her, Pauline fell down in shock, lost all memory. . .

After getting all the information, I came back to England, where I still had a problem to solve. I had asked my nurse not to give Pauline any clues. Did she remember anything? If so, would she love me? She seemed to be surprised to see me back. Anyway, she had come to. And between us a friendship was fostered. She began to sing and play the piano again. But was she aware of the meaning of her wedding ring? Keeping it on her finger showed that she did not dispute the fact that, somehow, she was wedded. Who could be her husband save me? Did she have no idea about it? Afraid of getting an answer from her, I delayed asking from day to day. But one day I noticed there was no ring on her finger. The meaning was only too clear: although she knew herself to be my wife she wished to throw the yoke aside. Then, I had to set her free. With much pain, I came to say farewell to her, when unconsciously I held her tight and kissed her. I saw the blush spread from her cheek to her neck before my very eyes. She had realized everything in an instant when we met. Since I had not said anything, she had removed the ring to set me free. She drew forth a ribbon which hung round her neck. Upon it were threaded the two rings. We were married in the true sense of the word. Blessed with children and happy, I am now writing this tale. "You don't tell enough of what you did and have always done for me!" says my wife. And this is the only difference of opinion that exists between us.

The Dickinson collection at the Jones Library was, at that time, on the top floor of the building. With just three small windows, and the weak light from the antique lamps, the room was dim. There were no other visitors, and I was alone in this quiet room. Turning over the pages of *Called Back*, whose pages were now dog-eared and whose binding was loose, I felt the spirit of Emily who had enjoyed the selfsame story more than one hundred years ago.

The story seemed like something out of a Harlequin romance. But written more than a hundred years ago, it had an antique flavor to it, and even sheer nonsense can have its own charm. Emily's work was always concise and she instilled a multitude of meaning in each word. So it was interesting to note that she had enjoyed this kind of story, one so different from her own literary style.

The only scholar who examined the meaning of this novel for Dickinson is Jerome Loving in his book, *Emily Dickinson*. According to Loving, what must have interested Emily was not the sentimental plot, but its use of blindness and amnesia, and the dilemma that Vaughan must *see* and Pauline must *remember*. Loving argues that Martha was not the only Dickinson to make sentimental use of Conway's title: Emily's sister-in-law, Sue, gave the title as "Called Back" when she submitted the following poem of Emily's to a publisher.

> Just lost, when I was saved!
> Just felt the world go by!
> Just girt me for the onset with Eternity,
> When breath blew back,
> And on the other side
> I heard recede the disappointed tide!
>
> Therefore, as One returned, I feel
> Odd secrets of the line to tell!
> Some Sailor, skirting foreign shores —

> Some pale Reporter, from the awful doors
> Before the Seal!
>
> Next time, to stay!
> Next time, the things to see
> By Ear unheard,
> Unscrutinized by Eye —
>
> Next time, to tarry,
> While the Ages steal —
> Slow tramp the Centuries,
> And the Cycles wheel!   (J160)

According to Loving, there is no doubt that the poet in this instance is being called back; however, it is not from death, but from the *idea* of death. It seems to me that Sue wasn't so far off the mark. Loving mentions that Martha doubtlessly interpreted the words to indicate Emily's expectation (and explanation) of death. She has chosen these words for Emily's epitaph and we are easily inclined to accept her interpretation.

One afternoon as I was reading the climax of *Called Back*, Marty Noblick, who monitored the library archives and whom I'd met during the course of my research and reading the book, entered the room with something to show me. "We have just acquired this," she said, handing me something carefully wrapped in cotton in a small paper box. It was a pair of cameo earrings with white silhouettes of a male and a female on a pale orange background. "These used to be the buttons on one of Emily's dresses. A person who got these from Madame Bianchi, that is, Emily's niece Martha, contributed them to us. So we can safely say they are authentic." The buttons had been worked into pierced earrings, which I touched softly. Many years ago, Emily had touched them, too. "Next time when we see them, it will be through glass." The two of us held our breath.

On another visit to the library as I was reading the last page of *Called Back*, it was close to five and the room was about to close. The approaching dusk grew denser and deeper. As I was leaving, I noticed the buttons already displayed in the corner of a glass case. The date of the acquisition typed on the card read "October, 1986." I already looked forward to when I would come back to this room in the Jones Library. Surely, the earrings would call me back to Amherst and to this very moment in time.

# Boston, 1987

I SPENT THE LATTER HALF OF MY FIRST YEAR IN THE UNITED STATES IN Boston, partly because I wanted to experience both rural and urban life in the United States and partly because Emily had visited Boston several times. Two of her visits were taken after her "reclusive" life began. She was twice treated in Boston for eye problems when she was in her mid-thirties. Considering that she rarely left Amherst, the fear of losing her eyesight must have been immense. Also, a significant number of her writings are housed in Cambridge and Boston. Emily's poem manuscripts are roughly divided in two; one half is at Amherst College and the other at Harvard University. The Boston Public Library possesses some of her letters, but they are very important ones.

I found lodging in Cambridge near Harvard. My apartment was also a few blocks away from Longfellow's House. This unexpected encounter was interesting because Longfellow was Emily's contemporary and his pre- and posthumous reputations have been utterly reversed, in stark contrast to hers.

Henry Wadsworth Longfellow (1807–72) was from one of Boston's distinguished families. He was a professor at Harvard and had a deep-seated knowledge of European culture. He left poems much loved by people, such as "Song of Hiawatha," "Paul Revere's Ride," "A Psalm of Life," "The Children's Hour," and "The Arrow and the Song." His popularity spread to Europe and also Japan, where they were eager to translate his works. Since then, his popularity has rapidly waned. He has been branded as didactic and conventional. Yet, the significant enthusiasm for his poems during a time when Emily's work was completely neglected is surely worth considering. Emily herself often cited his works in her letters. Today, there seems to be a movement to re-evaluate his work, especially the craftsmanship and natural flow of his prosody. A tour of his house, a visit to the blacksmith's house close by (see his poem, "The Village Blacksmith"), which now houses the Cambridge Center for Adult Education and its Blacksmith House poetry and fiction reading series, and lunch at the Wayside Inn in Sudbury (see *Tales of a Wayside Inn*, which includes "Paul Revere's Ride"), provided me with the chance to savor the poetic climate of Emily's period from a different perspective.

While looking at a map of Boston, I found that there was a statue of Edward Everett Hale (1822–1909) in the Public Garden. Among the addressees of Emily's letters was a Hale, who turned out to be the same man. When she was a teen, her father's office employed a law student named Benjamin Franklin Newton (1821–53). Nine years older than Emily, Newton was like an older brother to her; he introduced her to the world of literature and encouraged her to become a poet. After spending two years in Amherst, he moved to Worcester, Massachusetts. His death at the age of thirty-two was a great shock to Emily. In one of her letters she wrote: "When a little Girl, I had a friend, who taught me Immortality — but venturing too near, himself — he never returned —" (L261). This friend is commonly supposed to be Newton. Nine years after his death Emily wrote to Newton's pastor, Hale, to make an inquiry, beginning "Pardon the liberty Sir, which a stranger takes in addressing you, but I think you may be familiar with the last hours of a Friend" (L153). She wished "to know if his last hours were cheerful, and if he was willing to die" (L153); it was so crucial to her faith that she ventured to "transgress a courtesy" (L153) to write to a complete stranger. Hale's reply is not known to have survived, but several years later Emily sent another short note to him with a rose. As a distinguished minister and writer, he was already renowned during his life time. And as slight as this encounter might be, it shows that Emily was acquainted with a rich circle of contemporaries.

*Boston, 1987*

The statue of John Harvard at Harvard Yard is surely one of the most famous in Boston. It, too, can be connected with Emily. The sculptor, Daniel Chester French (1850–1931), who is best known for the Minute Man Statue in Concord and the Abraham Lincoln Statue for the Lincoln Memorial in Washington, D.C., came to work in the Berkshires every summer, and his studio, Chesterwood, is open to the public today. Emily is thought to have known French only briefly when he lived as a young boy in Amherst with his family; Susan Dickinson and the Norcross cousins were among his friends. Emily sent a letter to French upon the unveiling of the Harvard statue in April 1884:

Dear Mr. French: —
We learn with delight of the recent acquisition to your fame, and hasten to congratulate you on an honor so reverently won.
   Success is dust, but an aim forever touched with dew.
   God keep you fundamental!
                Circumference, thou bride of Awe
                Possessing thou shalt be
                Possessed by every hallowed Knight
                That dares to covet thee.
                                Yours faithfully,
                                Emily Dickinson   (L898)

In this poem (J1620), artists — that is, "hallowed Knights" — covet with awe circumference as their sphere. *Circumference*, which is also an Emersonian term, is one of Emily's favorite words. Once she declared, "My Business is Circumference" (L268). This word stirs the imagination and permits many interpretations since it is at the very beginning of the poem, placing it somewhere beyond time and space. Another one of her poems includes the word at its very end:

        The Poets light but Lamps —
        Themselves — go out —
        The Wicks they stimulate —
        If vital Light

        Inhere as do the Suns —
        Each Age a Lens

Disseminating their
Circumference —   (J883)

Emily hopes works of art will be appreciated more as time goes on, but with the magic of poetry, especially with the key word *circumference* in the case of the poem within the letter, the meaning is much more dynamic, deep, subtle. Out of context, the poem can be read as a description of aesthetic, erotic, or religious fulfillment. She sent the first poem to Otis Lord, presumably in the attempt to win his affection. It is an example of how Emily used her poems for different intentions, one of her great charms and mysteries.

A considerable amount of her archives are housed at the Houghton Library at Harvard. The building itself is not large but it has a European-style dignity and formality. The library allows entrance only to those who have a letter of introduction or a Harvard I.D. There is a room on the first floor where you can read manuscripts from Emily's family members — her parents' letters to each other, genealogies, correspondence of her brother Austin, letters Emily and her sister Lavinia received, etc. In a monitored exhibit room on the second floor, there are artifacts from her life — things such as her desk, a chair, a ring, and an embroidery sampler in a frame. The library houses not only a Dickinson collection but also collections related to the likes of Shelley, Melville, and others. The curators there have too many other valuable things to focus solely on the management of Dickinson archives, I'm afraid. In 1987, there seemed to be much work to be done. American Dickinson scholars also lament the lack of a Dickinson specialist there. Her manuscripts are kept in boxes; scholars are encouraged to consult Franklin's two-volume facsimile edition, as opposed to the originals.

In comparison, it is far easier to use the Boston Public Library (BPL), where Emily's archives are housed in a special room. You have to be qualified to enter the room, but once you enter they give you her letters for your perusal. You can read as many as you like. My time spent at the BPL was one of subdued stimulation of mind in a quiet atmosphere intruded upon by only three curators and a few other visitors.

I was very excited by the library's generosity and by seeing Emily's own handwriting, particularly her first letter to Higginson. Thomas Wentworth Higginson was a writer, minister, critic, and abolitionist who left the "Galatea" collection, which includes Emily's approximately seventy letters to him, such as the following, which is the first:

Boston, 1987

> Mr Higginson,
> Are you too deeply occupied to say if my Verse is alive?
>   The Mind is so near itself — it cannot see, distinctly — and I have none to ask —
>   Should you think it breathed — and had you the leisure to tell me, I should feel quick gratitude —
>   If I make the mistake — that you dared to tell me — would give me sincerer honor — toward you —
>   I enclose my name — asking you, if you please — Sir — to tell me what is true?
>   That you will not betray me — it is needless to ask — since Honor is it's own pawn   (L260)

This letter is one of the landmarks in the whole range of American literature, and here it was in front of me! It was dated April 15, 1862, when Emily was thirty-one. Having already written a considerable amount of poetry, she was so impressed with Higginson's lead article, "Letter to a Young Contributor" in that April issue of *Atlantic Monthly* that she wrote to him. Along with her letter, she enclosed her calling card and four of her poems. It is easy to imagine how much necessity compelled her to write, especially considering it was to a complete stranger. She was not part of any fashionable literary circles, and had not published any of her poems by her own will. Did the letter come straight from her heart, or was it literary maturity that consciously created the impression of urgency? No literary person would dare to refrain from answering such a powerfully intriguing letter.

Of course, Higginson did answer. Their correspondence lasted until her death and he visited her twice in Amherst. He sent his impression of one visit to his wife with this telling remark: "I never was with any one who drained my nerve power so much. Without touching her, she drew from me" (L342b). In Higginson's reply to Emily's first letter, he seems to have asked her a banal question, her age. Although his letters to her are not extant, she replied to the question with witty, twisted evasiveness: "You asked how old I was? I had no verse — but one or two — until this winter — Sir —"

When it comes to the issue of her poetry itself, Higginson did not and could not wholeheartedly support her idiosyncratic writing and irregular rhymes. When Higginson corrected these idiosyncrasies, she thanked him, calling his act "the surgery." She added, "it was not so painful as I supposed"; it seems that she was aware that her poems were unconventional.

And yet, although she never failed to thank him for his comments, she never took his advice.

Higginson, who judged Emily's poems as unconventional, felt she violated the poetic rules. The conventional poems of the period had a melodious meter, whereas her meter was "spasmodic" (L265). She was "uncontrolled" (L265) in many other ways: rhymes were not strictly followed — she often used slant rhymes; capital letters were employed more often than in ordinary usage; in most cases, dashes were substituted for periods and commas. After she died, Higginson compiled a collection of her poems with Mabel Todd. They did their best to make Emily's work "acceptable," modifying her strange habits of writing, sometimes even changing words to make them rhyme. To our eyes these "surgeries" have almost killed the poems; Emily was fastidious with her poems — what might seem to many as small changes which would have been monumental to her.

According to one theory, Emily is said to have put her dream of publishing in the hands of Higginson, who was not qualified enough to understand the true meaning of her poems. Thus, the subscribers to this theory are sorry that her book failed to be published during her lifetime because of Higginson's misjudgment. However, it is still questionable as to whether that was what she sought from him.

It is likely that Emily contemplated prudently whom to choose as her tutor. She must have thoroughly known the period's accepted style of poetry, especially from female poets, and that Higginson supported the conventional style, such as exemplified by Longfellow. It seems that she sought in Higginson some kind of external support, an objective eye to judge whether her verse was "alive" or not. Later she wrote to him: "you saved my Life" (L330). Despite the criticism leveled at Higginson for some of his reactions to her work, he was one of Emily's first editors to bring her to public attention, and as such he made an important contribution to her present level of acclaim.

While reading Emily's letters to Higginson at the BPL, I noted something interesting that could only be observed by looking at the original letters. In one, she reacted to one of her poems being published in a newspaper against her will:

> Lest you meet my Snake and suppose I deceive it was robbed of me — defeated too of the third line by the punctuation. The third and fourth were one — I had told you I did not print — I feared you might think me ostensible. . . (L316)

What she refers to here as "my Snake" is her poem beginning "A narrow Fellow in the Grass" (J986), which appeared in both the *Daily* and the *Weekly Springfield Republican*. "Robbed" is a shocking word that reflects Emily's indignation. Moreover she felt "defeated" when she saw the punctuation printed not as she had written.

Along with this letter, she sent a clipping of the poem from the *Weekly*. Emily generously gave the printed page to Higginson, although she might still have retained one from the *Daily*. Today, we can reproduce a printed page or even an entire book rather easily. Yet, before that, it was a dream for most amateur writers to see his or her work in print. Her enclosure of the clipping serves as evidence of her lack of attachment to the printed page, which may help to explain her self-chosen status as an unpublished poet.

As far as we know, nine other poems were published (one was published in a book) in her lifetime. An amateur poet might have collected his or her clippings. Nothing of the kind was in Emily's possession. It is surmised that they may have been lost, yet it is much more likely that the idea of saving the clippings never occurred to her. Also, she might have thought her poetry would be lost in the act of printing it:

> To see the Summer Sky
> Is Poetry, though never in a Book it lie —
> True Poems flee — (J1472)

For sixty years, Emily's works suffered all kinds of alteration. Moreover, the feud between the Dickinsons and the Todds resulted in the division of Emily's archives, followed by both sides publishing her work piecemeal. It also resulted in her archives being divided between Harvard University (where Austin Dickinson's daughter, Martha Bianchi, donated them) and Amherst College (where Millicent Bingham Todd gave them). It was in Thomas H. Johnson's edition of *The Poems of Emily Dickinson* in 1955 that the complete poems were presented to the readers for the first time. The result was a kind of "discovery" of the nineteenth-century poet in the twentieth century. And this delay has caused an unjustly low recognition of Dickinson in countries other than the United States.

In Johnson's edition, all 1,775 poems (according to his count) are arranged chronologically, grouped by year; at the end of each group, poems that were left unfinished are included. Emily seldom recorded the date of composition. In some cases, the poems were incorporated in letters with dates, but in most cases, handwriting analysis is the basis of the arrangement. Emily's handwriting changed conspicuously as time went on, which aided the difficult task of establishing chronology. But the time when she incorporated a poem into a letter was not necessarily the time when the poem was first composed. The more we think about her process, the more complicated things become. Johnson did his best, and it was an incredible amount of work.

Johnson's first edition includes the variants of what Emily left. In many cases, she didn't specify her preference for final word choice. The following poem is an illuminating example. The variants are given at the end of the poem:

> Shall I take thee, the Poet said
> To the propounded word?
> Be stationed with the Candidates
> Till I have finer tried —
>
> The Poet searched Philology
> And when about to ring
> For the suspended Candidate
> There came unsummoned in —
>
> That portion of the Vision
> The Word applied to fill
> Not unto nomination
> The Cherubim reveal —     (J1126)
>
> Line 4. finer = vainer / further
> Line 5. searched = probed
> Line 6. Was = just / when
> Line 8. There came = Advanced

For example, Emily wondered whether the fourth line should be "Till I have finer tried," or "Till I have vainer tried," or "Till I have further tried."

Many other collections of her poems followed Johnson's lead. For general readers, it may not be necessary to have a poem with its variants, but to appreciate Emily's true intentions, the variants are integral. When I was talking about this issue with Margaret Freeman, a Dickinson scholar, I used the word *workshop*. She asked me, "Then do you think her poems as kind of unfinished?" I don't. Rather, I think Dickinson regarded poetry as something ephemeral and only through writing in this way, by leaving variants, a part of it could be captured. Shelley once wrote that "when composition begins, inspiration is already on the decline, and the most glorious poetry that has ever been communicated to the world is probably a feeble shadow of the original conception of the poet." I think that Dickinson readers following all of the variants grope to find the right word alongside the poet and come closer to that "original conception." I realize that this was rather an intentional method by Emily to try to capture "the Vision." It is no wonder she did not like to see her poems in print. In order to be a published poet, she had to follow the conventions of print of the period, to choose one word out of many.

Modern technology made it possible to convey Emily's "vision" in a form closer to the original than even the Johnson edition. *The Manuscript Books of Emily Dickinson* by Ralph W. Franklin was published in 1981. During the years 1858 to 1859, Emily began to make booklets of fair copies of her poems, finishing the process some time between 1861 and 1864. Each booklet, or "fascicle," was constructed of sheets of paper punched with two holes and then threaded with string. There are 40 total fascicles, which contain about 800 poems all together. Franklin called them "the poet's completed books" and arranged them chronologically. Another 350 poems are on unbound sheets and are called "sets" — there are 15 sets. Previous editors had rearranged all of the sheets and Franklin worked to put them back into their original order. Although the arrangement of the poems within the fascicles and the sequence of fascicles themselves has been a controversial issue, the great importance of Franklin's edition is that all of the poems in the book are presented in facsimile. We can see each poem almost exactly as Emily wrote it — we can feel how each poem "breathes." Just as in her first letter to Higginson, she was so concerned whether her verse was alive or not, whether it "breathed."

In examining the facsimiles, one of Emily's idiosyncrasies can be seen more clearly: her arbitrary use of capital letters. At times, her handwriting makes it hard to discern whether she meant a capital letter or not. In the Franklin edition, you can see the actual size of each letter she wrote. In Johnson's printed pages, all of her dashes are presented the same way. But in fact, as the Franklin facsimiles show, the length and angle of each dash is different; some scholars even claim that the angles may indicated a high or low tone. Thus, the publication of the facsimile edition was truly another epoch-making event in the history of the appreciation of Dickinson.

When the first anthology was published in 1890, Emily was a poet of almost no renown. Yet new anthologies were published one after another up until the publication of the complete poems in 1955. And although in most, other than Franklin's, the poems suffered from many "surgeries," her voice still reached the hearts of readers.

# Museums and Meditations

IN ADDITION TO SEEKING OUT COLLECTIONS OF EMILY'S MANUSCRIPTS when I arrived in Cambridge, I set out to make a tour of the area museums. This tour would give me a chance to get to know the city by walking around. On the Harvard University campus alone, there are three art museums (the Fogg, the Busch-Reisinger, and the Arthur M. Sackler) and four museums of natural history (the Botanical Museum, the Museum of Comparative Zoology, the Mineralogical and Geological Museum, and the Peabody Museum of Archaeology).

I chose the Botanical Museum first. My guidebook said that the flower exhibits were not real, but models made of glass. Even though the photo in my book seemed so bizarre, I thought my curiosity would be satisfied by paying just a short visit. On the contrary, the actual models were simply astonishing and outstanding three-dimensional figures of flowers in bloom. Botanical specimens in most cases, dried and pressed, are two-dimensional and their color fades with time; but with flowers made with this lost technique nothing degrades. According to the museum, the coloring was a secret known only to the German father and son who made these specimens. Moreover, since they were made of glass, it was easy to make them bigger than life-size. For example, a flower and an insect were both enlarged, dramatically showing how an insect sucks the nectar. In one case, a glass bee was enlarged to half the size of a human palm. It felt almost as if Emily had seen these models. She left a couple of sensuous poems on this act:

> Come slowly — Eden!
> Lips unused to Thee —
> Bashful — sip thy Jessamines —
> As the fainting Bee —
>
> Reaching late his flower,
> Round her chamber hums —
> Counts his nectars —
> Enters — and is lost in Balms.   (J211)

---

> A Bee his burnished Carriage
> Drove boldly to a Rose —
> Combinedly alighting —
> Himself — his Carriage was —
> The Rose received his visit
> With frank tranquility
> Withholding not a Crescent
> To his Cupidity —
> Their Moment consummated —
> Remained for him — to flee —
> Remained for her — of rapture
> But the humility.   (J1339)

Overwhelmed by the number of specimens (there are around 850 on display of the over 3,000 they made) and their craftsmanship, I eventually moved on to the Mineralogical Museum next door. Here, in rooms with bright light streaming through the windows, the stones are displayed in big glass cases. Precious gems, such as diamonds and rubies, are also exhibited as natural stones, rather than as jewels. I much preferred to see them in this way. I enjoyed their colors and brilliancy without thinking about prices. Looking at the amethyst specimens, I thought of one of Emily's poems:

> I held a Jewel in my fingers —
> And went to sleep —
> The day was warm, and winds were prosy —
> I said "Twill keep" —
>
> I woke — and chid my honest fingers,
> The Gem was gone —
> And now, an Amethyst remembrance
> Is all I own —   (J245)

This poem is rather simple and easy to enjoy; yet it has an evocative power that forces readers to wonder what it is that the "I" in the poem lost. There are a range of possibilities: it could be childhood, a friend, a lover, God. Or it could be poetic inspiration, since the word *prosy* is derived from *prose*, which is opposed to *verse* or *poetry*. Once having lost it, does the poet lament that the object itself is no longer there? Or is it the loss itself — not a specific object — that is vivid? Is it the emotion left after the loss that is her "Amethyst remembrance"?

Whatever the loss might be, the vivid image of the words "Amethyst remembrance" induces readers to meditate. They are just two commonly used nouns, but once strung together, they have such power — one of the wonders of language. In characterizing Emily's poetry, people sometimes use the word *crystallization*. So many images and feelings are packed into each word that as a poem is read word by word, each word's power explodes and surprises. As each charged word bumps against the others, they give off sparks. In doing my Japanese translations of her work, I have to add some words to explain these sparks and these additions surely dilute the poems' cryptic power, diminishing the connotations that produce the sparks.

As a translator, I always have to face this kind of problem. However, reading foreign poetry in my own culture can also be a delight, especially when I read it with my students. One of my students was so moved by this poem, especially by the words *Amethyst remembrance* that he made what he called "poor attempts at *waka* in the spirit of this poem." Waka (or *tanka*) is a traditional Japanese poem that was first written over a thousand years ago.

Japanese verses are based on their syllable count, or the number of syllables they contain. Waka is a poem of 31 syllables, arranged in lines of 5, 7, 5, 7, 7 without rhyme or meter. His waka read:

| | | |
|---|---|---|
| Murasaki-no | (5) | A maiden sleeping |
| Tama-mote-nemuru | (7) | Holding a gem |
| Otomego-ni | (5) | Of violet color |
| Omoide-wa-ari | (7) | Remembrance is with her |
| Asa-wa-aketsutsu | (7) | The day dawning |

While some people pull back at the very thought of reading foreign poetry in a foreign language, this student did not. In recasting an English poem into a Japanese verse form, he went right to the point of reading poetry in a non-native language and culture; he took his native language and culture into account.

In Emily's poems, there are not only ordinary stones like pearls and rubies, but also uncommon ones, like chrysoprase and chrysolite. To use jewel imagery was a literary fashion of the period. One of her favorite poets, Elizabeth Barrett Browning, for example, also employed such imagery. But in Emily's case, reasons beyond literary fashion might have been at work as well. Her scientific education at the Female Seminary was much advanced for the time. Another source of inspiration is The Book of Revelations, which she named as one of her favorite books of the Bible; it is replete with jewel imagery.

I enjoyed every museum on the Harvard campus, and the many others in greater Boston. Especially noteworthy was the Isabella S. Gardner Museum. Gardner literally "made" the museum. She collected the works, designed the building, and raised the funds to operate it. Her home, an Italian-style villa that eventually ended up as the museum, seems like one huge greenhouse. Upon entering, you are welcomed with a mass of flowers in the courtyard and seized by the illusion of a dreamland.

In purchasing the works of art, Gardner took the advice of Bernard Berenson, an art critic studying in Europe at that time. As a result, her personal collection is extraordinary. I could not help but be transfixed when I found Vermeer's "The Concert," which is the only Vermeer in Boston — even Boston's huge Museum of Fine Arts is without one. (Back in Japan I was surprised to read in the newspaper that the painting had been stolen in 1990. Its whereabouts are still unknown today.) In one of the rooms on the first floor are displayed articles left by artists, Liszt and Brahms to name a few, with whom Gardner was friends. In one of the displays, I found a picture of a white fox and a letter by Tenshin Okakura (1862–1913). In the latter half of the nineteenth century Japan underwent modernization and westernization but Tenshin advocated that we should not lose sight of the significance of tradition in Japanese art, something that Ernest Fenollosa championed in the west. After founding the Tokyo Art School, he was invited to the Museum of Fine Arts in Boston to head its Oriental section. While he was in Boston, Gardner befriended him. "White Fox" is a poem he wrote in English.

Browsing through books in the museum shop, I found a list of the intellectuals who had corresponded with Gardner. My eyes were running over it carelessly, when I came across a familiar name — T.W. Higginson. It was quite unexpected, but quite natural that they were acquainted with each other since they were members of the same intellectual circle in Boston. Higginson invited Emily to come to Boston several times and Gardner might have been the very person who embodied the most flamboyant side of that fashionable circle. How different it was from the quiet world of Emily's Amherst! Through the correspondence between Gardner and Higginson, the uniqueness of Emily's world became more obvious to me.

The Gardner Museum was completed in 1903, more than ten years after Emily's death. But Gardner had been reigning in Boston society much earlier than that. Born just ten years after Emily, Isabella Stewart married into the Gardner family, one of Boston's most distinguished families. But society was cool to her since Boston's upper crust felt that she was an upstart, that she married into her position. After spending several years in Europe, Gardner found confidence in herself. Her salon flourished. In the museum, I could almost feel her tenacious desire to hold Europe in her hands. It is reported that she declared, "I am an American. Once I have bought a picture, it can never go back to Europe." When Gardner acquired Titian's "Rape of Europa," Berenson told her, "You have acquired Europe." Gardner used her great wealth to defy Europe and the Boston society that had snubbed her. But the United States was just beginning to find value in its own culture. It is not too surprising that Emily, who lived in a small rural town utterly unrelated to Gardner's fashionable world, found meaning in her own America rather than Europe. Emily's sense of America was acquired through quiet observation, in complete contrast to the confident defiance of Gardner. And when it comes to intensity, Emily's might be stronger:

> The Robin's my Criterion for Tune —
> Because I grow — where Robins do —
> But, were I Cuckoo born —
> I'd swear by him —
> The ode familiar — rules the Noon —
> The Buttercup's, my Whim for Bloom —
> Because, we're Orchard sprung —
> But, were I Britain born,
> I'd Daisies spurn —
> None but the Nut — October fit —
> Because, through dropping it,
> The Seasons flit — I'm taught —
> Without the Snow's Tableau
> Winter, were lie — to me —
> Because I see — New Englandly —
> The Queen, discerns like me —
> Provincially —      (J285)

Emily chose the robin, the buttercup, the daisy, and snow to represent New England, while the cuckoo and the nut represent Britain. She claimed that she was equal to the queen, since both have their own preferences that are developed according to each's environment. If Emily is "provincial," then so is the queen. The word does not only mean "local" but it has a pejorative connotation as "rude" or "crude." Yet Emily does not look down on the queen either. Instead, she revels in the sense that they are peers. How daring and poignant a last line!

# The Art of Calligraphy

THE NOTION OF CONSIDERING HANDWRITING AN INTEGRAL PART OF A poem is a familiar one in Japan. According to *The Tale of Genji*, when nobles exchanged poems (especially love poems) in the eleventh century, calligraphy and choice of paper contributed to the meaning of each poem. This tradition is still alive; poets, especially haiku or tanka poets, take handwriting quite seriously in their work. The presentation is just as important as the content. Thus, the artistic ability of calligraphers has great value.

Cambridge's continuing education center was near where I lived and I found that some of its offerings interested me, especially a course on calligraphy. However, I was in Boston to complete my research so my time for other pursuits was limited. All the same, it was rather difficult for me to resist the temptation to take calligraphy.

I had been taking Japanese calligraphy lessons for quite a while and I was gaining a sense of how broad and deep this art was and how hard it was to pursue. With calligraphy, it is easy to feel as though you are making no progress, no matter how hard you try. It is an art that requires much devotion, time, and energy. I tried to talk myself out of the temptation: If I have time to try Western calligraphy, I should devote that time to the Japanese art. If I get too absorbed in Western calligraphy, my already sloppy attempts at Japanese calligraphy will only become sloppier.

However, in my mailbox in the English Department of the Harvard Graduate School of Arts and Sciences, I received a guidebook from Harvard Neighbors, an organization whose aim is to help newcomers and their families adapt themselves to their new surroundings. An events calendar was included: it listed a tea party at a member's home, lectures, and gatherings for several kinds of hobbies, including calligraphy. Alas, I could no longer resist. I justified it as another good opportunity to get to know Harvard better. I told myself that as I placed a call to the instructor whose phone number was listed in the booklet.

The instructor, Kitty Pechet, informed me that she was not going to offer her calligraphy class that term, but we did talk for several minutes about why I came to Harvard. The following day, I unexpectedly got a call from her.

"Would you *really* like to learn calligraphy?"

She had decided to offer her class. She was encouraged that I had taken Japanese calligraphy lessons in Japan, that I understood the discipline that the art required. And she was swayed by the fact that I was in the United States to study Dickinson and wanted to write her poems in calligraphy; she said it was a strong motivation. She said, "How can I refuse?" When she was young, our instructor hoped to be a painter and once studied with Oskar Kokoschka, a German expressionist known for his portrait paintings. What she learned from him was to see with your own eyes. Later on, when she got married, she began to do calligraphy as something she could do more easily at home.

The office of Harvard Neighbors was located in the basement of one of the buildings on campus. I was surprised to find that of the ten people gathered in the classroom, half of them were Japanese. The five Japanese women were in the Untied States with their husbands, who were affiliated with Harvard to perform research. It seemed that I was the only beginner, but I felt comfortable with my classmates since I found in them good friends.

We began by learning Carolingian style, which was developed during the reign of Charlemagne (circa A.D. 750–900). This style has no capital letters, so we finished the lowercase alphabet in four or five lessons. I was enjoying this new skill so much that I made sure I found time to complete the homework in my hectic schedule. And I cannot forget how contented I was when I finished writing one of Emily's poems for the first time in Carolingian script. I also enjoyed the atmosphere of the class and the time at the end to chat with my classmates. I mentioned that I was here to do research on Dickinson; one of the other students brought me a magazine article on her and another gave me a small illustrated book of Emily's poems.

All of the students were very good calligraphers. Our instructor told the other students not to expect to learn as quickly as the Japanese students, since many of us had already studied the tradition of Japanese calligraphy. And I was grateful for that tradition. Although Western calligraphy and Japanese calligraphy are very different, the basic idea of writing beautiful characters remains the same. In order to achieve this level of skill one must study carefully, consult a copybook, and practice; the demands of calligraphy teach us not to be in a hurry.

About halfway through the course, our instructor arranged for a field trip to the Houghton Library. On the Harvard campus, the library houses Emily's archives along with other precious collections, including old manuscripts. Generally, the collections are not easily accessible, but since we were students of the calligraphy course sponsored by Harvard Neighbors, we were granted access privileges. One of the rooms in the library was specially prepared for us. We viewed some absolutely fabulous manuscripts and listened raptly to the curator's stories about them. Many of the Renaissance manuscripts dated back several centuries, others from a millennium ago. It was breathtaking to see the Carolingian script in its original form. The variety of styles of letters, kinds of paper, and colors of ink were used at a time when mechanical printing had not yet been invented. It was undeniable that each piece we viewed was created with immense energy and by a creative mind. It was irresistibly alluring.

The pleasure of pouring over old manuscripts was not new to me. When studying Japanese calligraphy, we examined the characteristics of documents from different periods. By transcribing the works as precisely as possible, we studied the brush stroke and practiced our calligraphy. The manuscripts were often divided into separate pieces of paper, mounted, and displayed in museums all over Japan. It was an added pleasure to make trips to various museums and cities to encounter each work. And you saw what you could not observe on a printed page — the brushwork, the texture of paper, the composition of the work as a whole.

*In Search of Emily*

After completing the Carolingian letters, our instructor had us copy a Roman manuscript all with capital letters. I tried, following the examples on the photocopy she gave us, but there were several A's and each A was a little different from the others. Wondering which A I should take as the standard, I asked the instructor to let me know which letter form I should copy. She replied, "Didn't I give you the photocopy the week before? Look at it and try it yourself." I was chagrined that I did not take the time to actually see the manuscript photocopy with my own eyes; I was too focused on quickly acquiring the superficiality of form. I now realize that this is something that I must watch out for. We Japanese are skillful enough to learn something new efficiently and quickly — the modernization of Japan as a result of Meiji Restoration is most probably due to this facet of our culture — but I think we lose a lot during the process, individually and communally, by not using trial and error and not seeing with our own eyes.

Toward the end of the course, as the final assignment of the term, each of us was to create a booklet. We could choose any theme we liked and we were to give attention to its visual composition. We bound our booklets with string, and shared them with the rest of the class. An elderly student, a beginner like me, had made little progress, but she always looked very happy in the class, and her booklet was filled with that same happiness. Another charming classmate was from the Netherlands and her technique was not as good as the Japanese students in the class, but her booklet was full of pictures and colors and her letters danced, which was exactly what she was like.

Our last class fell on the day before the opening of an exhibition of our instructor's work. The show was all set and the class previewed the work. It exploded with exquisite kaleidoscopic changes of colors and shapes. For example, a poem with the word *lavender* in it was written in lavender ink on a sheet of light lavender paper. An intense poem by Welsh poet Dylan Thomas about his father's illness — "Do not go gentle into that good night" — was expressed in dark brown, solid letter style, and violent brushwork. The variety of colors was different from Japanese calligraphy, which employs only neutral paper and black ink, relying on the subtle differences in its shades of gray. It was so nice to see these examples of what she had tried to get us to put into practice.

My booklet included three Dickinson poems in Carolingian style: I included "To make a prairie it takes a clover and one bee" (J1755), "Where Ships of Purple — gently toss —" (J265), and the following poem, along with my translations of them into Japanese:

I died for Beauty — but was scarce
Adjusted in the Tomb
When One who died for Truth, was lain
In an adjoining Room —

He questioned softly "Why I failed"?
"For Beauty," I replied —
"And I — for Truth — Themself are One —
We Brethren, are," He said —

And so, as Kinsmen, met a Night —
We talked between the Rooms —
Until the Moss had reached our lips —
And covered up — our names —     (J449)

"Beauty" and "Truth" are personified by vivid images. The vast range of eternal time is presented in a concrete description — until the moss covers up the tombstones. It is one of my favorite Dickinson poems because the meaning is so profound, allowing dichotomous interpretations on art and life. And even though these "characters" are abstractions, in the poem they become vivid, concrete, and lifelike. In my calligraphy, I placed small, blue dots around the word *Beauty* whenever it appeared, and placed yellow-green dots around the word *Truth*. At the end of the poem, I used both blue and yellow-green dots to show that beauty and truth have melted into each other. I looked forward, one day, to acquiring sufficient skill in calligraphy to represent another interpretation of this poem, one nearly opposite to the one I presented — that is, both beauty and truth have fallen into decay. The challenge was learning how to express this ghastliness in a beautiful form like calligraphy.

# Amherst, 1993

SIX YEARS AFTER MY FIRST STAY IN AMHERST, MY WISH TO RETURN WAS granted by a fellowship from the American Council for Learned Societies. First, applicants' papers were screened. Then, the director of the American program in New York came to Japan to conduct one-hour interviews with each applicant who made it through the initial screening. Candidates were interviewed individually about why and what each wished to study in the United States.

Although I had only been teaching at Osaka Shoin Women's University for just two years, I was granted special permission to take leave. Through the experience of my first stay, Amherst had become my second home and I missed it. I also wanted to continue my research on Emily's home. So at the end of the academic year in March 1993, I wrapped up my affairs and arrived in Amherst in early April. The winter was rather severe that year, and snow could still be found on roads. When the bus stopped at the Amherst Common, my heart was filled with the thought that I had made it — "I have come back at last."

And yet, there was no time for sentimentalizing: first and foremost, I needed to find suitable lodging. For the first week, I stayed at an inn called Emily's B&B, which was named, of course, after her. Shortly thereafter, I rented a room from a couple whose tenants had come from all over the world. I was told that a Japanese boy had left just before I arrived; a Malaysian boy had been there for two years; and a Japanese girl came and went for short stays. They were thoroughly accustomed to Asians, but I was teased for being the first Asian tenant who hadn't brought their own rice-cooker.

As small, quiet and rural as it is, the town of Amherst had experienced some changes in my first extended stay (in 1986–87), most of which were in the downtown area. Pizza was now very popular. Students were now satisfying their appetites for under two dollars, including a drink. They could be seen daily, sitting on the stone stairs downtown, devouring pizza. The employees of the most crowded pizzeria, taking orders from customers briskly, shouted out, "Who's next?" "Who's next?" At first, I hesitated to join in with my awkward English, but I soon got the knack of regularly "grabbing" a quick slice of pizza.

Restaurants featuring Asian foods were also new to Amherst. Non-traditional uses of Japanese ingredients like *miso* or *somen* had made their way to this small town in Western Massachusetts. An upscale organic grocery store, some twenty-minutes from town, provided a variety of foreign foods. Among other items, they stocked an array of Japanese seaweed — not only *kombu* and *wakame* but also *arame* as well as *hiziki* — a rarity in small supermarkets in Japan.

The bookstores had also changed — I continued to hunt for children's poetry books since I found them to be good introductory readers for my Japanese students. Soon after my arrival in Amherst, I found an antique shop in front of The Homestead. A white dress, napkins, and laces were displayed in the window — distinctly Victorian, like Emily. The store also dealt in used Dickinson books. The prices were reasonable and it became one of my pleasures to visit the shop, spending time and money on pretty things just as I used to. The owner eventually became a friend of mine. One day, after having bought one of her Dickinson books, I went to the post office. The man at the window asked me, "You just bought a Dickinson book, didn't you?" I stared at him in round-eyed wonder. He turned out to be the antique shop owner's husband.

Since my research and interests are mainly in the literary field, I am afraid I am not always observant of changes in society. Yet some did not elude me. For example, I was pleased to see that recycling was more popular than it was six years ago. Once a week, blue plastic boxes packed with old newspapers could be seen in front of each house. The colleges were also sensitive to this movement, proposing various new methods for recycling and reuse during my relatively short stay.

To observe all these minute changes and to have personal interactions with the locals is surely one of the delights of living in a small town. For this, my second extended period of living and working in the United States, I could have chosen any town or city. I was tempted to live in New York City. That would have been interesting and exciting. However, all things considered, I chose to return to Amherst and the decision was a good one. I found a myriad familiar faces, and I never felt lonely. And my comfort with the coziness of the town helped me to forge new relationships.

During this year-long stay, I was able to explore more. And I learned, for example, that Amherst takes advantage of its small size, functioning efficiently and providing an endless stream of events and activities, many of which are supported by volunteers. For example, the guided tours at The Homestead are conducted by volunteers. All the astronomy programs — observatory sessions and planetarium shows at Amherst College, and solar observing on the Amherst Common — are held weekly by the Amherst area amateur astronomers association.

I also discovered a group called "Round the World Women." This association was established after a tragedy when a foreign woman, who had come to live in Amherst because her husband had been transferred here, killed herself out of loneliness. Now the members, wives whose husbands have vocational or research positions in Amherst, meet twice a week. They complete everyday tasks such as going to the post office or enjoying dinner together. They are not necessarily good at English, which often is a main reason why it is difficult for them to find friends there. As a result, they also participate in special English programs as well. The organizing, planning, and transportation for this group is taken on by local women in Amherst, all volunteers. These volunteers enjoy developing friendships with people from all parts of the world. Through this group, I was introduced to many other Asian women, one of whom happened to live next door. Without the program, I would never have met these friends or learned quite so much about Amherst and American life.

When flowers were in bloom, I also took part in a garden tour. Map in hand, my landlady from my previous stay six years before, who was now a very good friend, and I toured several different gardens — one was on the top of a hill with a lovely, scenic view; another was a Japanese-style garden. Each of the gardens had its own charm, and all had such beautiful arrangements of flowers. The homeowners had opened their gardens to complete strangers — some even invited us in so that we could get a different view of their gardens from inside their houses. I am afraid that the Japanese are not as open as this. Here, people kindly answered questions by visitors. For the owners of the gardens, it was a kind of volunteer work. However, I'm sure they enjoyed showing off the results of their years of hard work, which encourages them to continue their efforts.

Inspired by the spirit of volunteerism in Amherst, I decided to participate myself. The Teddy Bear Rally on the Amherst Common was sponsored by the Rotary Club and held on the first Saturday in August. There were nearly two hundred booths where teddy-bear-related goods were sold. Those who had teddy bears at home brought them to show them off — some people drew carts filled with bears, while others paraded proudly with huge bears in their arms.

For fund raising, booths sold food and T-shirts. That year's shirts had a picture of a bear and a basketball on them since the Amherst High School girl's basketball team had won the state championship that year. More than a month before the rally, when the shirts arrived, I was assigned the task of folding them. On rally day, I worked as a saleswoman. As nervous as I was, after the first few customers, I began to enjoy the job of selling. I found it also served as a good English lesson because the limited vocabulary and expressions were repeated again and again. Observing how veterans were waiting on customers, little by little, I acquired expressions like, "Yes, it may shrink a *little*." It was a joy to give them advice and to see customers satisfied with their purchases.

I volunteered on another occasion and was pleased to unexpectedly learn more about the workings of the town. Amherst was establishing relationship with Kanegasaki, a town in the northern part of Japan. Officials were coming for a formal signing of the agreement, and I accompanied the group during its two-day visit. The friendship between the two towns started with an exchange program between their junior high schools.

In all the time I spent in Amherst, this was my first visit to its Town Hall. I also had a chance to meet town officials for the first time and got to know a little about the political system of the town. Amherst does not have a mayor; it is governed by a five-member select board and 240 town meeting members.

In both bodies, about half of the members are women. When I met the Japanese delegation, one of the first things that came to mind was its lack of women. I could not resist asking about it. The answer was that it was impossible, for no woman was in a position to chair a town assembly or to be a superintendent of education in Kanegasaki. As expected, Amherst women raised an outcry for the Japanese delegation to include women next time. This is an issue not only in Kanegasaki, but all over Japan. The ratio of women among the members of Japanese assembly ranks 110th among all the countries in the world. Japan is still a male-dominated society. And it is not only men, but also women themselves who are not comfortable with females in the political arena. As I completed my two-day volunteer duties, I wondered how long it would be before the number of Japanese women in the exchange program equaled that of the Americans.

With my Dickinson studies as my main focus, I was not always as observant of Amherst society as I could have been. But a second opportunity to enjoy life in this small town gave me the chance to enjoy the changes and become involved. I was moved by the spirit of openness and volunteerism that made Amherst such a comfortable and dynamic place.

# A Literary Landscape

LIVING IN AMHERST AGAIN ALSO GAVE ME THE OPPORTUNITY TO VISIT many more literary sites in and around the area: the Concord of Emerson, Hawthorne, Thoreau, and Alcott; Emerson's Lexington; Melville's Pittsfield; Hawthorne's Salem, Mark Twain and Hariett Beecher Stowe's Hartford and more. It gave me an enhanced sense of the literary climate in the vicinity of Emily's Amherst.

In addition to discovering the mark other poets and authors left on the surrounding townships, I discovered other writers in Amherst, such as David Grayson and Eugene Field. Also, locals are most proud to point out that Robert Frost was an Amherst poet. Born in San Francisco, Frost spent much of his time in New England, mainly on his farms in New Hampshire and Vermont. From 1916 to 1962, just a year before his death, Frost was associated with Amherst College (either teaching or lecturing or giving readings) and thus came to be much connected with the town. I saw a photo of Frost captured during one of his informal teaching sessions with his Amherst students: it was as if young people were listening to the teachings of an old sage. I thought that perhaps it was an image from bygone days, when poets were thought of with reverence. Yet when Seamus Heaney came from Ireland to give a poetry reading during my stay, Johnson Chapel at Amherst College was overcrowded and I found many students leaning forward and listening intently. I could not help but remember the Frost picture — here, at least, the tradition was still alive. In 1962, Amherst College named its new library for Frost. While in Amherst, Frost stayed either with his friends, at the Lord Jeff Inn, or at one of seven other residences. All of these places were near where I was living; one that he had owned was on the same street. It was impossible to go to the library or walk downtown and not think of him.

I heard that Frost's poem "Fire and Ice" was written when he was in Amherst. It's an eschatological poem (about the end of the world), and is, thus, very serious; yet it is written in easy, almost colloquial English and in perfect rhyme. Little did I dream that I would often be in the very house that had seen that poem's birth.

Although New England summers are generally nice and cool (compared to Japan), the weather can get really muggy. My landlord, an architect, allowed me to work on my word processor in his air-conditioned office in a three-story, grand, white house built in Colonial Revival style. One day, he told me that Frost had written one of his most famous poems in this space when he rented the house from 1918 to 1920. I was dumbfounded but thrilled to learn that I had been working in a place of such historical significance. I eventually learned more of the house's history, which included an incredible move. In 1989, the 92-year-old building housed apartments and the local newspaper's office. The town of Amherst planned to demolish it in order to build a new police station on the site. To save the historic house, it was put up for sale for just $1 — because the move was estimated to cost over $100,000. My landlord decided to buy the house for his new office and take on the Herculean task of moving the building. On March 23, 1989, the house was moved from 109 to 401 Main Street. The process took an entire day. While inching down Main Street it snagged an over-hanging branch, but that obstacle was easily overcome. "I was the hero of the day!" my landlord beamed with pride. Though the shuffling of houses from one place to another was not new to Amherst, the thought of this big house moving slowly past the Dickinson homestead struck me as fascinating and humorous. Emily, who used to observe the hustle and bustle on Main Street from her windows, would have surely enjoyed this show and the people who gathered to watch it.

When the Summer Institute for Dickinson was held in 1990 in Amherst (at the Marsh House near the Evergreens), about twenty high school teachers from all over the United States joined the three-week program. On the weekends, we carpooled to places of interest nearby. On one of these occasions, I had a chance to go further west in the state to Tanglewood in the Berkshires to enjoy an open-air concert. On our way, we visited a few other places. Having checked my guidebook, I suggested we visit Cummington to see the William Cullen Bryant Homestead. The other passengers were not entirely enthusiastic, but reluctantly agreed simply because there was no reason to object. The house was situated on a hill, and as the car went up, we all began to get excited. When we looked down from the top of the hill, the view spread before us was superb: a green hillside sloping down and ridge after ridge receding into the distance. Everyone uttered a cry of joy, since no one had expected this. I was relieved, for I felt responsible for having dragged them to this place. The house, which was grand, was unfortunately closed (since it is open to the public only during a certain times of year), but the beauty of the scenery dispelled any disappointment.

I had always hoped to go back to see the inside of the house and have a tour. The scenery itself would be worth a second visit. In early fall of 1993, I found an article in the local newspaper about a craft show to be held at the site; the house would be open. I decided to go there when there was a walking lecture along the poet's trails in the nearby woods. When I got there I saw more than one hundred craft booths, which would explain the need for such vast site. It was a clever idea to have a craft show in that environment, given the gorgeous landscape. After strolling among the craft booths, I took a tour of Bryant's house.

Although this house was not his birthplace, it was his boyhood home. When he was an older man he eventually purchased and renovated it, and it served as his summer retreat from 1866 until his death in 1878. There were many exotic artifacts since Bryant was a world traveler. After touring the house, it was interesting to walk on the paths on which he had walked and touch the trees he might have touched. Ahead of his time, he maintained the importance of keeping fit by walking at least three miles a day.

On a snowy day in winter, the Hitchcook Center in Amherst offered a program on Bryant as a landscape architect. I had to walk all the way there, plodding through the snow to the center, but it was a good, informative slide show and lecture. Bryant helped found Central Park in New York when he was a journalist there, and his funeral at the park attracted a huge number of mourners. Bryant's foresight into the significance of having such a huge park in the rapidly developing megalopolis of New York was admirable. He brought his concept of New England nature to the city. My adventure brought me closer to the New England scenery, and it became more and more familiar to me until I felt at home surrounded by it.

In her letters, Emily cited Bryant's "Thanatopsis" and some other poems. In the following poem, she showed a special kinship and reverence to him, calling him "Mr Bryant":

> Besides the Autumn poets sing
> A few prosaic days
> A little this side of the snow
> And that side of the Haze —
>
> A few incisive Mornings —
> A few Ascetic Eves —
> Gone — Mr. Bryant's "Golden Rod" —
> And Mr. Thomson's "sheaves."
>
> Still, is the bustle in the Brook —
> Sealed are the spicy valves —
> Mesmeric fingers softly touch
> The Eyes of many Elves —
>
> Perhaps a squirrel may remain —
> My sentiments to share —
> Grant me, Oh Lord, a sunny mind —
> Thy windy will to bear!    (J131)

Her theme here is the transition between autumn and winter. "Mr Thomson" is the British poet James Thomson. His quartet work titled "The Seasons" was well known in New England in her day. Bryant's "Golden Rod" can be found in his poem "My Autumn Walk":

> On woodlands ruddy with autumn
>     The amber sunshine lies;
> I look on the beauty round me,
>     And tears come into my eyes.

> For the wind that sweeps the meadows
> > Blows out the far southwest,
> Where our gallant men are fighting,
> And the gallant deed are at rest.
> The golden-rod is leaning,
> > And the purple aster waves
> In a breeze from the land of battles,
> > A breath from the land of graves.

These are just the first twelve lines out of the 64-line poem, in which Bryant addresses natural themes as well as human concerns, such as war. The goldenrod and the aster are paired again in the third stanza of another poem by Bryant, "The Death of the Flowers":

> The wind-flower and the violet, they perished long ago,
> And the brier-rose and the orchis died amid the summer glow;
> But on the hills the goldenrod, and the aster in the wood,
> And the yellow sunflower by the brook in autumn beauty stood,
> Till fell the frost from the clear cold heaven, as falls the plague on men,
> And the brightness of their smile was gone, from upland, glade, and glen.

Here again is the combination of nature and humanity, although the focus is shifted from the former to the latter, since the last stanza is about "one who in her youthful beauty died" and "perish[ed] with the flowers." It is possible that Emily had this particular poem in mind as well.

After my first year in Amherst in the 1980s, I returned to my teaching in Japan and decided to read *Ethan Frome* by Edith Wharton with my students. Since I had weathered a winter there in town, I felt far more qualified to explain typical Yankee reticence and the temperament of New Englanders. During my second stay in Amherst, the film version of Wharton's *The Age of Innocence* was playing in theaters. Friends of mine kindly proposed a trip to The Mount, Wharton's summer house in Lenox, Massachusetts. Born into a wealthy New York family, Wharton spent her summers in that huge, Georgian-style country mansion. That turn-of-the-twentieth century house boasted an elevator. It was interesting to hear a tour guide discuss how Wharton wrote: often she was in bed, surrounded by scraps of paper.

What was also wonderful about The Mount were its indoor and outdoor theaters. We had reserved tickets and enjoyed two short plays based on

Wharton's short stories. The performance was held inside The Mount, an ideal setting with its limited number of seats. The experience of seeing plays in this atmosphere was unforgettable, all the more so because the house and the garden were designed in part by Wharton herself. We enjoyed a picnic on the premises, eating our supper and taking a nap. We enjoyed another play, A *Midsummer Night's Dream*, performed outside under the sky. The opening was spectacular with players dancing in from the woods. The two couples of lovers, dashing and mingling, making the most of the wide, open space, expressed the full spectrum of human passion as intended by Shakespeare. At the close of the play, it was midnight. Looking up, we saw the bright moon in the sky, and the actors at the windows and on the balcony of The Mount waving. We answered with our applause.

Back in Amherst, when I saw the movie *The Age of Innocence*, I realized that the movie was better than my imagination in visualizing Wharton's fashionable New York — the gorgeous mansions, costumes, and meals. When I discovered a poster at the Jones Library for a talk by a Smith College graduate who had helped in the preparation of the food for the movie, I was happy for the chance to get a rare glimpse at a few of the secrets behind making a feature film. The lecturer explained that it required a lot of research to decide what kind of food to make and what utensils they used. An enormous amount of work was done just for each brief shot. Watching the slides depicting extravagant tableaux of decorations and food, we uttered sighs of recognition and admiration. Later, we enjoyed some samples of period food.

Several years later, I compiled a textbook in Japan called *Romantic Women Poets*, containing about fifty British and American poets. Inspired by my experiences in Amherst and at The Mount, I chose Edith Wharton to serve as the anchor. Like Dickinson, she was modest about her poetry, but even in her early teens, she wrote poems of considerable quality.

Arriving again in Amherst in 1993 at the beginning of April, I could enjoy summer fully for the first time and realize why Dickinson praised this season most enthusiastically. Coming from a home literally in the middle of a city in Japan, I appreciated life in Amherst and close contact with nature all the more. I could see how people liked gardening and devoting their free time to this all-important conversation with the earth. Fortunately, I, too, could feel this sense of unity with nature. My landlords had a spacious farm, where they grew flowers and vegetables. I helped them when I could and frequently accompanied them to their booth at the farmers' market, held every Saturday during summer on the Amherst Common. I had sometimes visited the market in the past to buy fruit and vegetables and had come to know the familiar faces behind the booths and each one's specialties, such as flowers, homemade cookies, or bread. Now, I went almost every week, not only to buy things, but also to help sell.

During strawberry season, we drove back and forth several times from the farm to the market to sell strawberries. As I helped with the laborious task of picking the berries, they joked it would help me understand Emily better. In fact, she did write one poem about strawberries:

> Over the fence —
> Strawberries — grow —
> Over the fence —
> I could climb — if I tried, I know —
> Berries are nice!
>
> But — if I stained my Apron —
> God would certainly scold!
> Oh, dear, — I guess if He were a Boy —
> He'd — climb — if He could!   (J251)

Upon first reading, the poem may seem too childish to be treated seriously. That might be the reason why it has seldom been addressed in critical work. Then a feminist reading shed new light on it: the consciousness toward the limit and restraint pressed on women can be found in a girlish sigh. Margaret Freeman, a Dickinson scholar, suggested another reading: this "I" could be a boy. It's entirely possible, for Emily adopted a male persona in at least one other poem, and little boys also used to wear aprons at that time.

One summer day, I was fascinated to find a tussie-mussie in a glass in the kitchen of the house where I was staying. A tussie-mussie is a small bundle of flowers fashionable in the Victorian era. Each flower represented its own message, a combination of which was sent to a lover or a friend. Hoping to make one, I had not dared to practice with the expensive flowers sold in flower shops in Japan. Here, there were plenty of flowers on the farm. Emily had her own garden, and she sent flowers in her letters quite often to friends. However, a typical tussie-mussie was too big to be enclosed in a letter.

On another summer evening at a Dickinson program, one of the participants suggested an evening visit to Emily's garden. I followed along, not expecting more than a chance to glimpse her garden in the twilight. When I arrived, however, I was grateful for the suggestion. Small lights floated here and there — fireflies! A well-known poem by Japanese poet Izumi Shikibu (circa 970–1030) came to my mind:

> *Mono omoe-ba*
> *Sawa-no hotaru-o*
> *Wagami-yori*
> *Akugare izuru*
> *Tama-ka to-zo miru*

> When I watch
> a firefly on the marsh
> it seems almost as if
> it were my soul issuing
> from my body in longing.

"Longing" is inevitably part of love according to the verse tradition of the period. Yet, whenever I think of this poem, I regard the word in a broader sense: the soul confined in body longing to be liberated. Watching fireflies in Emily's garden, I was sorry that she had not written any poems about them.

When the summer season was at its height, I could hear the music of insects. In the tradition of the Japanese literature, poets have praised the beauty of this music. When I heard one or two singing at the door of the house, I wondered why the sounds of insects were not usually treated as beautiful in Western literature. But in the deep woods of Amherst, with all the insects singing at the same time, keeping me awake, I came to understand.

Fall in New England is simply splendid — so much so that people from all over travel there to enjoy the changing foliage. The autumn leaves in Japan have their own delicate beauty, but their beauty is on a grand scale in New England.

Winter came, but the snow was rather slow in arriving. There were only three days of snow before Christmas, and it had melted away rapidly. People began to yearn for snow. Emily herself expressed this longing in one of her poems, "Without the Snow's Tableau / Winter, were lie — to me —" (J285). But on Christmas morning, we awoke to find a blanket of white snow! Walking outside, I listened to soft exhalations as hard powdery snow struck the branches of the trees. I saw grains of snow fall like glitter. When the temperature dipped very low, the snow froze fast to the branches. As the winds blew hard, the ice came pelting down with clattering music. I found that the landscape had as much music in its snowy state as in the summer. And the candles in the windows of some houses provided light and a sense of warmth as I trod home in the evenings.

    Shortly after New Year's Day, all the shelves of greeting cards at the stationery shops and supermarkets went through a complete change to bright red hearts for St. Valentine's Day. The shelves changed again for St. Patrick's Day, and that space was, just a few days later, occupied by Easter cards. Even though it might have been the middle of February, the stores were already prepared for early April. The bright spring colors of those cards gave me a presentiment of the coming of spring and at the same time some sadness, for I had to leave Amherst at the end of March. They made me think how quickly another whole year in Amherst had passed.

# Celebrating Emily

THE TOWN OF AMHERST IS NOW, FOR ME, A SORT OF HOMELAND OF MY soul. I feel so at home there because it is the town of my most beloved poet. And during my prolonged stays in Amherst, an endless stream of Dickinson-related events kept my days full and kept me too busy to be homesick.

Upon my return to Amherst in 1993, I paid a visit to the Jones Library. The year before, it had been under renovation and it was almost finished. With the official reopening events over, the library was back in full swing. The building was now much more spacious, with a reading room in the center that admitted lots of glorious sunlight through a large skylight. The Special Collections Department that houses the Dickinson archives had been completely changed. I thought it was a bit of a shame that those old rooms with their antiquated atmosphere were now lost, but the new space was excellent. With far more room than before, the new department has room for its exhibits on Dickinson, Frost, as well as an entirely new one on Robert Francis. Emily's life can be traced through pictures and texts: in the glass cases were manuscripts of her poems and letters and memorabilia, including the cameo buttons I first saw seven years ago. A display of the poems published during her lifetime, assembled together for the first time, was the result of a special effort: copies of the newspapers that carried each of her poems can be seen all at a glance. (Karen Dandurand's scholarship brought that number up from seven to ten poems.) There was also a videotape player with which you could view videos on Dickinson and Frost. There was also a reading room, and a stack room beyond that. And the Special Collections were not only archives for poets, but also for town history and genealogy. I enjoyed observing both old and young people researching their roots.

Within a month after my arrival, I was given an opportunity to give a talk at The Homestead on translating Dickinson into Japanese and on the reasons why she is so loved by the Japanese people. The resident curator, Carol Birtwhistle, had written to me while I was still in Japan, asking me to speak to the tour guides. It was a great honor to talk to a group of people who already know Dickinson so well.

In my talk on translating, I covered four points. First, how the translated poems could be "poetry" when the rhymes and rhythms are, in most cases, not translatable into Japanese. Secondly, compactness — one of the charms of Dickinson — is often lost in translation. Her beauty sometimes results in seemingly ungrammatical English (since it deviates from normal syntax) — which cannot be transferred into equally ungrammatical Japanese. The result is often a lengthy Japanese translation. Thirdly, since the Japanese language (spoken, in particular) has ways of denoting gender, Dickinson is often translated (mainly by male translators), using the female style, which I try to avoid. Finally, I discussed the difficulty in interpreting Dickinson due to the cultural differences.

People assume that Japanese like Dickinson for a variety of reasons. The Japanese Emily Dickinson Society, which was established eleven years before the American (or International) one, is one reflection of Japanese interest. Another is that many scholars from Japan participate in Dickinson conferences. Also many Japanese visitors come to The Homestead. However, Dickinson is well-known only among the scholarly world; among the general public in Japan, she is far less popular than Poe and Whitman. That said, what is it that attracts the Japanese audience to her? Haiku, a short form of poetry in Japan, is often cited, since most of Emily's poems are short. For traditional haiku, it is mandatory to have *kigo* (a word designating one of the four seasons), and similarly Dickinson often takes up nature in her poems. However, to find affinity easily is a dangerous thing. Beauty is surely what both Dickinson and haiku have in common. Still, when it comes to the quality of this shared characteristic, it should be treated carefully. Moreover, since haiku (a five-seven-five syllable poem) are derived from another short form verse, tanka (a five-seven-five-seven-seven syllable poem), the difference of the two forms should be clarified to find a closer affinity to Dickinson. Personally, I have always been interested in the affinity in calligraphy. The facsimile edition of her poems has allowed a broader audience to examine her manuscripts, and the notion of handwriting as being an important part of the poetry is an easy one for the Japanese people to accept.

After the talk, I went home only to realize that I had left my notebook behind. When the resident curator saw me when I returned to The Homestead, she kindly took me to the cupola; I had never been in the small room since it is not included on the guided tour. I wondered whether Emily had come here often to be completely alone or to command a nice view of the entire town. The curator also took me to Emily's bedroom, saying, "I know you want to see this when people are not around." It was a rainy day. The lamps in the room were on, and as I talked about Emily with her for perhaps half an hour, the soft light mingled with the murmur of the rain. In that short time, I got a glimpse of what it would have been like to spend a rainy day in that quiet room.

May 15th is the anniversary of Emily's death. On the Saturday closest to that date there is an annual walk to the cemetery where she is buried. I was happy that for the first time I would be around to participate. Emily left explicit instructions for her funeral — she asked to be carried out the back door, around through the garden, through the opened barn from front to back, and then through the grassy fields to the family plot. The annual walk retraced this burial route. That year, the Unitarian Universalist Society sponsored a program called "The World of Emily Dickinson" during the anniversary walk weekend. The event was thronged with people. Each participant placed a flower on her grave, some recited a poem or two, and others talked about their personal relationship to Emily. Here I met an old friend of mine, Joann Duncanson, who had composed music to Emily's poems. She sang the poems as she accompanied herself on the guitar. Her songs are in the folk style, easy to enjoy and sing. This time, she presented her joyous new work — a copy of a small picture book called *The Story of Emily Dickinson*, a story she sang and to which we could respond with a short easy refrain. The three-day event also included *The Belle of Amherst*, a well-known one-woman play about the Emily's life, and a lecture by Martha Ackmann, a professor at Mount Holyoke College.

The end of July brought the beginning of the annual meeting of the International Emily Dickinson Society. The society was established in 1990, and this was the first time the meeting was held in Amherst. It offered participants the chance to see The Homestead and explore the other Dickinson sites. One of the associated activities was a slide lecture on The Evergreens, Austin Dickinson's house, by project manager Greg Farmer. The local Da Camera Singers gave a performance in which they sang Dickinson poems set to music and also sang popular music from the period, including hymnals, the Scottish traditional "Comin' thro' the Rye," the Irish melody "'Tis the last Rose of Summer," and "Yellow Rose of Texas." The latter is often referred to as perfect to be sung with Dickinson's poems.

With such wonderful summer weather, the annual meeting was held in Dickinson's garden under a large oak tree. After the keynote address and reports, lunch was held. The Dickinson conference gave me the chance to talk to doctoral candidates about their research and to meet scholars whose names I knew only through their published writings. I was almost star struck. I wish I could have talked with each one of them about his or her book.

In September, when the school term started, I found a course on Dickinson being offered during the fall semester at Amherst College. Such an offering is, in fact, very rare. Although Dickinson is an integral part of courses on American poetry, or American Romanticism, she is seldom treated alone as a theme or subject of a course, even among the five Amherst-area colleges. Professor Karen Sanchez-Eppler presented a well-crafted syllabus for the course. Along with Dickinson poems and excerpts from the critical studies on her, other period works were also on the required reading list. The latter provided a better understanding of Dickinson's literary and cultural environment. Taking advantage of being in Amherst, the class scheduled visits to The Homestead and the Frost Library. At the Frost Library within the college, the students saw Dickinson's manuscripts for the first time. They were surprised and excited and obviously hadn't taken into consideration that these manuscripts were housed at Amherst College.

In early October, I was invited by Professor Gary Lee Stonum to attend a symposium at Case Western Reserve University in Cleveland, where, again, I talked about translating Dickinson from English to Japanese. Another panelist at the symposium, Ann Sherif, discussed translating prose from Japanese to English. We thought our talks would complement each other well. Having studied Japanese and having been to Japan, Sherif understood Japanese sensibilities very well. We hit it off immediately. Before the symposium, I asked her to allow me to audit her Japanese class. She hesitated and declined with a wonderful Japanese expression *"Omise dekiruyouna monodeha arimasen"* (This is not something worthwhile to be seen, I'm afraid). When Japanese decline, we usually don't offer a direct "no," which is often regarded as impolite. Her manner of declining let me know that I could be allowed to attend the class.

I was back in Amherst on December 10, Emily's birthday, and it was a momentous and somewhat unfortunate day. About a week earlier, the curator at the Jones Library had told me he had a big piece of news concerning her. One of her manuscripts, a poem beginning with "She sped as petals" (J991), had previously been categorized as "missing" in the authoritative Johnson edition of *The Complete Poems of Emily Dickinson*. The manuscript was found and now put up at auction at Sotheby's. On discovering this, the curator of the Special Collections, Daniel Lombardo, checked how much the library could afford to bid on the manuscript. He was ready to join in the bidding by phone. He wanted it badly for the library. And I did, too. There were not that many suitable places for Emily's manuscripts. Sadly, he didn't succeed and was truly disappointed; in a short time the bidding price had risen tremendously — and prohibitively. I was so sorry to hear it and could find no words for consolation since there is a little chance that another "missing" manuscript will turn up any time soon.

The interest in looking at Emily's own handwriting has recently increased greatly. Although we can enjoy the printed form, that does not at all lessen the importance of the original manuscript, especially for scholars who specialize in her. But the primary hope is that her manuscripts, wherever they may be kept, will be easily accessible to us all.

# Simsbury High School

At the beginning of May 1994, I spent two weeks teaching at Simsbury (Connecticut) High School at the invitation of a teacher at the school, Marilyn Strelau. I initially met Strelau when she attended the Summer Institute on Dickinson for American high school teachers in 1990. I had joined in the program along with another Japanese Dickinson scholar. Strelau asked me to visit her school. I would observe and then I would participate in classes on American Literature, Poetry, Multicultural Literatures, the Short Story, and Japanese.

In Strelau's American Literature class, we read Dickinson for a special extended period of two weeks — a rare, generous amount of time to devote to just one writer. Taking advantage of her experience at the Summer Institute, Strelau showed slides that she had made and played a videotaped monologue she had written and performed about Emily's life. She encouraged her students to write poems using Dickinson's first lines, such as "We learned the Whole of Love —" (J568) and "Surgeons must be very careful" (J108). That assignment resulted in some admirable and unique poems. I lamented that in Japan high school students are not often asked to do creative work like this.

I talked to the students about translating Dickinson, read some translations aloud for them to hear the Japanese, and distributed photocopies of the translations for them to see how the Japanese characters looked on paper.

When we first began to deal with Dickinson, I discovered that most of the students had a stereotypical image of her as "a recluse" and "a death poet." Since death is an integral theme in her poems, it was rather difficult to dispel this stereotype wholly. The students seemed estranged, not from her poetry, but rather from her lifestyle. These extroverted American students had trouble identifying with her introverted ways. Later Strelau reported to me that in their answers on the examination, the students referred to Dickinson as "Emily," like she was someone they knew. Both Strelau and I were pleased that we had brought them that feeling of intimacy.

During one of our discussions on how to present Dickinson to the class, Strelau remarked, "Emily barely published her works. I think she was unfair not to share." It reminded me of something Helen Hunt Jackson once wrote to Emily urging her to publish: "It is a wrong to the day you live in, that you will not sing aloud" (L444a). In the United States, it is not at all wrong to put yourself forward as much as you can and aim to be famous. Considering this ethos, Emily's preference to avoid publication and fame might be somewhat incomprehensible, especially for high school students full of hope for the future. One of the students very seriously asked, "Can we become famous later if we stay home, write poems, and never publish them?"

Compared with Americans, Japanese people are introverted enough to better understand Dickinson's lifestyle. One Chinese scholar even finds Orientalism in Dickinson, comparing her to Chinese poets who did not seek fame, but were satisfied with honest poverty. This kinship might be one of the reasons why the Japanese like Dickinson. However, as the Japanese phrase goes, "Those that look alike are often completely different." This superficial affinity could be, in fact, a big difference. The Japanese avoid speaking out in order to maintain harmony with others. Thus, they lose individual identity. Dickinson, on the other hand, holds her individuality deep inside. She chose to withdraw in order to define herself more precisely.

The poetry class, an elective course, was for seniors only. I participated in two poetry sections in which there were, relatively speaking, many students, and the teachers conducted their classes briskly. For example, one of the teachers asked the students one by one to speak briefly, according to their seating order, about what they thought about the Dickinson poem they just read. Some of the students simply said whether they liked it or not; others gave some penetrating insight concerning the theme of the poem. One student said, "Dickinson's poems are a waste of paper." It struck me that sharing these opinions, whatever they might be, can be useful and important. In Japan, students are often too timid or too afraid of making mistakes to speak freely.

The teacher asked me, "What do you think about the students who said they don't like Dickinson?" I said to the students, "You cannot satisfy everyone. So it is quite natural that some people like Dickinson and some people don't. However, what I want to ask you to keep in mind is that I hope you won't hate poetry itself simply because you don't like one poet. You are sure to come across poets you like, or you may come to like Dickinson in the future even if you do not like her now. To come across poets you don't like is also an important discovery for you. To know which poems you like and don't like, to know which poets you like and don't like, are ways to know yourself better. These preferences become a method of self-discovery."

The Multicultural Literatures course was started by Strelau in 1991. Knowing that Simsbury was overwhelmingly white, she wanted her students to know more about other cultures. To have a course on multiculturalism at the high school level and to be ready to invite a person like me, not only to observe but also to conduct classes, struck me as a very positive attitude. Although I was not sure how much I could do and wondered whether I served as an adequate representative of Japan, I believed that meeting a native was a better experience than any of their books could provide. For many of the students, I was the first Japanese person they had ever met.

At the beginning of the course's unit on Japan, students were allowed to ask me questions. They ranged from "Are there McDonalds in Japan?" and "How are American teens different from what you anticipated before you came to the States?" to "What is the Japanese system of government?" All of the students were eager to learn about Japan. I really wished I'd had more time to answer them at length.

I demonstrated several aspects of Japanese cultural heritage: the kimono, flower arranging, the tea ceremony, calligraphy, and origami. Some critics might say selecting these activities is no longer a good way to introduce Japan to foreign countries and that focusing on these things might further emphasize the stereotype of exoticism. And yet I felt nothing interesting would happen from merely stating that all human beings are the same. I would have

*In Search of Emily*

liked to talk about the Japanese automotive or high technology industries, but I have, however, no expertise in those fields. I am interested in art and culture, and I hoped to demonstrate how these traditions are a part of ordinary, modern Japanese life.

Strelau also asked me to make a reading list for the short story course before I left Japan. We exchanged several letters and agreed on assignments that included works by Naoya Shiga (1883–1971), Yasunari Kawabata (1899–1972), and Kobo Abe (1924–93). I had proposed a volume from *The Tale of Genji*, and it was rejected. Strelau felt that the teenagers would not like it since it is too tedious, too slow in its development. I had expected this. Still, I regretted that we could not read it since Japanese culture could safely be said to have culminated in *Genji*, or at least a large part of it is represented in this work. Instead, Strelau chose *Patriotism* by Yukio Mishima. Although I acknowledge his talent, I fear this selection too easily satisfies Westerners' curiosity about what *they think* is Japanese. It presents the "Japanese things" to the foreign eye that are easily comprehended within the bounds of Western aesthetics. In the classroom, the impact of Mishima's story was deep, and it prompted many questions. Although I had previously declared that I didn't like the story and was appalled by its cruelty, I found it ironic that a lot could be explained through this story. In the end, I was surprised to find myself almost defending Mishima. The ritual aspects of Japanese culture and the Japanese spirit, lost to an easy willingness to worship Western culture after the war, are well depicted in his work.

It was wonderful to help expose high school students to Japanese literature through these courses. When it comes to the trade of translation, Japan has imported far more than it has exported. The number of Japanese works translated into other languages is deplorably small. The teaching aids that Strelau showed me listed many works of Japanese literature in translation, including picture books and stories about Japanese traditions and culture. I was concerned, however, by the fact that so few of these works were done by Japanese writers or artists. Many of the authors or illustrators were American or Chinese; although in some cases they were nisei or sansei, second- or third-generation Japanese immigrants, many of whom did not retain their Japanese first names or family names.

At the end of my two weeks in the Multicultural Literatures course, there was an exam. One of the questions Strelau asked was, "What color or which sound would you associate with Japan and why?" Some of the students gave simple answers like, "I think of red because of their flag" or "blue because

Japan is surrounded by the sea." Others gave more thoughtful answers like, "Gray would be a color that I would associate with Japan. Gray does not stand out, is not bold, and this seems to be what the average Japanese person seems to be like. There is little individuality or boldness in the Japanese. Also, gray is an earth tone and Japan has an attachment to nature." Another answer neatly summarized one Japanese characteristic: "The Japanese have two voices at the same time, *honne* and *tatemae*, what a person really thinks and what the individual speaks out of the official position of the group he or she is in. I would associate Japan with the color of green because green is a mixture of yellow and blue. Yellow to show that you are happy outside. And blue because inside you are concealing something of yourself or family. The Japanese as I learned have two faces: one for outside the house (yellow) and the other for inside (blue)."

Another question on the exam was, "Complete this simile/metaphor with a nature image: Being Japanese is as. . . or being Japanese is like. . ." One of the responses contained a marvelous image: "Being Japanese is like a flock of birds, each depending on the other to keep a perfect harmonious formation in the sky." Another response was witty: "Being a Japanese is like feeling a breeze in a rice field with a computer on one's lap." I felt that the Japanese could learn from Americans about ways to cultivate more imagination and initiative in students.

Another one of the students said his impression of Japan was as follows: "Being Japanese is like a lion always looking for prey. The Japanese don't know when to stop; they just keep coming." I sought out his answer to the question, "What impression of Japan do you now have?" He wrote: "My impression of Japan has changed. I have come to realize that they are very much like us. Although I am still bitter about their bombing of our beloved Pearl Harbor, I can't bring the past into play." It was good to know that his impression had changed, and yet I found what I had expected.

Seven years ago in Amherst, there was a person who uttered "Remember Pearl Harbor" whenever he saw me. I never did reply, but I always debated with myself whether I should say something in response. In the end, I decided that to retort "No more Hiroshimas" would have been as worthless and disgraceful as his remark. Around that time, an acquaintance advised me to talk with an historian who taught at UMass. Professor Richard Minear was an expert on atomic bomb literature about Hiroshima, and he also translated *Requiem for Battleship Yamato*, a first-hand account of a Japanese battleship sent on a doomed mission at the end of World War II. Wondering whether he, too, had suffered similar verbal attacks, I asked him, "Since you do this kind of work, don't some Americans say to you 'Remember Pearl Harbor'?" "There are weirdoes everywhere," was his quick response. This remark, and my growing familiarity with people with idiosyncratic or iconoclastic viewpoints fostered by American society's emphasis on individualism, eventually softened any hard feelings these verbal attacks would provoke.

When I visited Minear another time, he gave me a draft of his latest paper, which was written about the Holocaust. In 1993, statistics showed that twenty percent of Americans did not believe that the Holocaust had actually occurred. To counter this perception, in the same year, the Holocaust Museum was created in Washington, D.C. It has been receiving far more visitors than had originally been estimated. In addition, Steven Spielberg's film *Schindler's List* had just been released and was very much on people's minds. In his paper Minear acknowledged the significance of the museum, but he also noted that "the United States chooses to commemorate the Nazi holocaust but not the atomic holocaust. Why? The Nazi holocaust is someone else's doing, not ours. Hiroshima and Nagasaki are *our* doing, not someone else's." When some Americans consider Hiroshima and Nagasaki from this viewpoint, I, as a Japanese citizen, in turn think about what we did to other Asian peoples in that and previous wars.

Discussing the nuances of Japanese culture with the students gave me the opportunity to think more about them myself. For example, "yes or no" questions are rarely employed by the Japanese. Hearing them used so often in the United States took some getting used to, and it seems be rooted deep in the difference between the two cultures. At least superficially, human beings are not all the same. And when superficial differences are taken out of context, they appear outrageous.

I talked to the students about American individualism versus Japanese groupism. ("Harmony should be maintained" is one of the clauses of the first constitution of Japan, declared about fourteen hundred years ago.) I then talked about American straightforwardness or directness versus Japanese subtlety or indirectness. When I told students at Simsbury High School that a Japanese "yes" could be "no," they looked utterly incredulous. But after President Clinton had talked with the Prime Minster of Japan, he left behind a memo given to him by one of his staff members which read, "yes means no." This incident happened shortly after my arrival in the United States. I heard from a friend that it was a hot topic in Japanese newspapers for a while. The fear is that some might think the Japanese are liars, but this needs to be put back into the whole context of Japanese culture. For example, a host(ess) asks a guest, "How about a cup of tea?" The guest answers, "No, thank you. Please don't trouble yourself," but perhaps thinks that "A cup of tea would be good, but I don't want to trouble the host, who might think me presumptuous if I ask for it." The host takes everything into consideration — that the guest must be thirsty having come all this way, that making tea won't be much trouble, that drinking a cup of tea won't, after all, be such a big deal, or that the guest might think me stingy if I can't even spare a cup of tea — and makes tea. The guest accepts the tea gratefully without any protest like, "I meant it. I really don't need tea." In Japanese culture, in which others are always considered in relation to yourself, everything is not expressed. You have to understand what is not explicit.

What is interesting is that this concept of "straightforwardness versus subtlety" also corresponds to the relationship between male and female speech. Japanese males will utter a definite "yes" or "no," while Japanese females don't give a frank "no" since they are afraid to hurt others' feelings. Summing up this complex issue like this might be simplifying too much, but it does make the "Japanese yes means no" more understandable.

Within Japanese culture the lack of an "empirical," or direct, Western approach is not a problem. Instead, we operate under the technique of intimation: without mentioning much, somehow anyone can communicate his/her views. When it comes to arguments, however, it is usually seems easier to persuade an opponent using Western techniques since the Japanese way of arguing is not meant to defeat an opponent. In Japanese society, the avoidance of conflict, especially the avoidance of conflict for conflict's sake, is interpreted as a kind of wisdom. Instead of a clash of wills there's an effacement of will in the service of the cause for dispute. In Western eyes it might seem contradictory, but it has its own "logic" and creates a certain sense of "identity" for the combatants — paradoxically, in this case identity is gained by giving it up.

I tend to acclimate smoothly to American life. I never get homesick, never experience culture shock, never long for Japanese foods. Oddly, people often say to me casually, "You look so happy here. Why don't you stay and live in the States?" That question seems presumptuous to me, almost an insult or a sign of ignorance, although I do realize that I adapt well to American culture and that this remark is intended as a compliment. I don't consider myself extraordinarily patriotic, yet I do have a sense of being more strongly Japanese when I am in the United States. I want to be treated as a

*In Search of Emily*

Japanese woman. I don't want to affect an American manner superficially, and I don't want to sell my Japanese soul.

I read an interesting article in the *New York Times* during this stay. It was the twentieth anniversary of Maestro Seiji Ozawa working with the Boston Symphony Orchestra. Part of it read as follows:

> His presence in Boston's wider musical community has been scarcely felt at all... Mr. Ozawa is a gifted teacher of young musicians, but most of his efforts in this area go to the school and festival he founded in Japan... After more than 30 years in this country, he still speaks English with difficulty... At heart, he remains, as he acknowledges, a visitor here... He will probably return to Japan, he said, where his children grew up and his wife still lives.

Ozawa is a person who is always conscious of his identity as a Japanese man and he thinks highly of his roots. His children were brought up in Japan. He preferred that they have a strong Japanese identity, even at the great cost of separating his family. I was surprised to read what I perceived as criticism of Ozawa in the article. I had expected Bostonians to be far more broad-minded and sophisticated. It reminded me of something else: without enough brides, farmers in the Japanese countryside have begun to "import" them from the Philippines. It was reported in Japan that when one of the brides sang a Philippine lullaby to her little baby, her husband and in-laws prohibited her from doing so. They didn't think to respect her culture. They didn't think that getting to know her culture would broaden their own. Was Ozawa being criticized for singing Japanese lullabies?

This issue of maintaining your identity in a foreign country is keenly felt every day, especially by a person like me, for whom language is not simply a means but a goal. The days I spent fighting with language were frankly days of humiliation. Occasionally, I have been asked to make speeches at international conferences, which for me is a tremendous task with what feels like insurmountable handicaps. First, there is the language barrier. In a scientific field, a mathematical formula could be enough to persuade an audience. In literature, language is everything. And then there is the cultural barrier. The Japanese are not accustomed to expressing their opinions or to making presentations in front of large audiences. The Japanese avoid making eye contact since looking others in the eyes is construed as awkward and embarrassing. Zeami (1363–1443), the greatest Noh playwright and actor said, "To hide is the essence." Basho (1644–1694), the grand master of haiku, wrote, "To express all of yourself. What's the point?" When I am asked to make a speech at an international setting, I simply panic. Nevertheless, I have been supported by the goodwill and magnanimity of my fellow American scholars, and I am pleased with their responses.

I am very conscious of my identity as a Japanese woman, and I belong to an older generation, which, I think, is more conscious of its Japanese identity than the younger generation. Some members of the younger generation who study abroad maintain their Japanese essence. They hold fast to their solid Japanese identity, and at the same time learn English and an American approach to life. I expect much of them, for it is up to them to represent the Japanese character to Westerners. One hundred years ago, Japan began enthusiastically absorbing and acquiring aspects of Western culture. Now Japan has to think about not only "importing" other cultures, but also "exporting" the Japanese culture to share with the rest of the world.

At the end of my stay in Connecticut, Strelau and I chose a Dickinson poem to summarize my experience. Emily refers to individuals in the following poem, but it could also apply to our countries and our cultures:

> We introduce ourselves
> To Planets and to Flowers
> But with ourselves
> Have etiquettes
> Embarrassments
> And awes    (J1214)

# Inspired by Emily

THE LAST TIME I CAME TO AMHERST, I HOPED TO PURCHASE A SET OF etchings by Margaret Taylor. She had just published in 1986 *From Amherst to Cashmere,* which combined selected poems by Emily Dickinson with ten of Taylor's own color etchings. It is a beautiful book, bound in silk and boxed. The illustrations only measure about two by three inches each, yet the subtle colors she chose are very attractive and give them a fuller, richer feel.

One of the benefits of living in a small town became clear when within weeks of my arrival in Amherst, I went to a book signing where I ran into Taylor. She told me about an upcoming exhibition of her work in Northampton: a collection of her large oil paintings. When the exhibition was over, we met for lunch one day and I got to know her better. Taylor had previously lived in New Mexico, but New England beckoned her. The fact that she had come to Amherst from a place with a complete different landscape made it possible, I think, for her to value the uniqueness of New England.

*Inspired by Emily*

In her Dickinson book, I was most attracted to the subtle light in each rendition of landscape, which I assumed only an Amherst resident could capture. Although her oil paintings were on a different scale and based on different subject matter, I could detect something in common with her etchings: You could still feel the air. I was intrigued by her unique and interesting interpretations of Emily's poems from her point of view as an artist.

A mutual friend, Betty Bernhard, who is a Dickinson scholar, gave me the courage to ask Taylor if I might buy one of her etchings since the whole set — a limited edition of fifty — was far beyond what I could afford. When I finally had a chance to visit her home studio and talk to her about the process of making the book, I asked whether she would be interested in selling her etchings individually. She said of course, and I ended up purchasing two. One was an etching of clouds blazing in gold and purple. A Dickinson poem was printed to the left of the image on the sheet:

> Blazing in Gold and quenching in Purple
> Leaping like Leopards to the Sky
> Then at the feet of the old Horizon
> Laying her spotted Face to die
> Stooping as low as the Otter's Window
> Touching the Roof and tinting the Barn
> Kissing her Bonnet to the Meadow
> And the Juggler of Day is gone     (J228)

The other etching I bought was inspired by the poem beginning with "A Light exists in Spring" (J812). Taylor showed me several versions of the same picture — blue was the predominant color in one, pink in another. Each etching seemed completely different.

In another etching, Taylor addressed the following Dickinson poem:

> White as an Indian Pipe
> Red as a Cardinal Flower
> Fabulous as a Moon at Noon
> February Hour —     (J1250)

An Indian pipe (its Japanese equivalent is "foreigners' pipe") is shaped exactly like a pipe as both names indicate; the plant is very small and wax-white — exquisite and ethereal, while a cardinal flower is blazing red. This poem defies interpretation, but Taylor's etching offered an admirable solution — against a snow-white background she etched the red bark of trees.

The owner of Emily's Bed-and-Breakfast, where I had stayed for the first week while looking for lodging, called me one day to tell me about one of her guests at the inn, a woman from Arizona who made sculptures inspired by Emily's poems. Her name was Barbara Penn, and I took advantage of the opportunity to meet her. I had often heard about pictures and paintings inspired by Emily's works, but the only sculptures I knew were Joseph Cornell's box works, which were exhibited in Japan in the early 1990s. This invitation whetted my usual interest in looking at visual interpretations of her poems.

We met at the Jones Library and we quickly became good friends. We often had dinner together and enjoyed reading poems by Robert Francis at the library. We talked about how we had come to know Emily and the challenges we faced as teachers. A booklet from one of her exhibitions deemed her sculpture "plastic arts." For example, one of her works consisted of boxes attached to walls, twenty-five neatly mounted in rows of five. In one box was an egg and in another a picture of an angel's wing. She used only earth tones — white, beige, brown, and black. I was filled with expectation about how Penn would interpret Emily's poems in her sculptures. Interestingly, she picked poems that were not the most well known or most often anthologized, such as:

> Best Gains — must have the Losses' Test
> To constitute them — Gains —    (J684)

She showed me her latest work, a piece titled "I Make the Yellow to the Pies" — a phrase taken from a letter Emily wrote to her cousin Louise Norcross. I was surprised that such an unpoetic and non-evocative phrase inspired Penn. In a written explication of this work, Penn described the work as a "large sculptural piece in pale yellows partially reconstructs the hive of the honey bee drone, whose life is an endless round of repetitive tasks" that illuminated Emily's "incongruous relationships to household and gender relative to the nineteenth century societal mandate for women," a mandate that provoked Penn's irritation at the scant amount of time allotted to women for creative work. Penn showed me photos of another work in progress — several earth-tone jackets hung on a wall. This piece, she explained, was inspired by the phrase "Option Gown" in one of Emily's poems. She asked me whether this was a phrase Emily had coined or if there really was something called an option gown around that period. That phrase in itself was surprising and I was pleased to have yet another stimulus to think about Emily that had never cropped up before — at least, for me.

One day, a Japanese woman who had been living in Amherst called me. She asked, "I am going to take another Japanese female scholar to Concord. Do you want to join us?" Since I neither drove nor owned a car, this offer was impossible to refuse. I inquired, taking advantage of her good will, "Can I ask an additional favor from you? Can we make the day Sunday?" I had heard about a bit of performance art, a special program on Sundays at the Colonial Inn: Belinda Hackler, dressed up as Emily, winds her way through the tables reciting Dickinson's poems and answering questions from the guests.

At the entrance of the dining room, we found Hackler in a white dress sitting on a chair. We sat down to lunch while Hackler walked among the other tables. When all of the other guests had left, she joined us. We asked her to recite some poems, while I provided their Japanese translations. Hackler told us that many of the guests who stayed at the inn or people who had lunch there had no knowledge that this program existed. "At first they respond to my acting with surprise or mild refusal, but soon they find themselves enjoying it. It's a job worth doing," she said. We agreed as we had had a wonderful time.

Brian Marsh, an Amherst area playwright and actor, wrote a theatrical piece, "The Search for Emily." I caught a performance of it. Marsh attempted to explore conflicting images of the poet. It was particularly fun to see Emily's meeting with Higginson (who was portrayed by Marsh on stage). Soon after, when I was visiting the Jones Library, I noticed that the woman behind the book check-out counter seemed familiar. As I drew closer I remembered where I had seen her before: She played the role of Lavinia, Emily's sister, in Marsh's play. When I finally came up to the counter, I excitedly exclaimed, "Vinnie!" Glad to know someone recognized her, she introduced herself by her real name, Kay Lyons, and that initial exchanged blossomed into a friendship.

One day, as closing time approached as I was working in the Special Collections room at the Jones Library the curator had a guest. Usually there were not that many visitors and most who came were interested in Emily, or the two Roberts. So I was slightly curious to know more and it did not hurt that from time to time I could hear the curator's enthusiastic exclamations such as "This is really marvelous" and "I have never seen such a wonderful thing" and an older woman's dignified voice. Giving in to the temptation to join them, I

*In Search of Emily*

got up and approached them. Glancing down at the paintings on the desk, I cried out, "Barbara Cooney," before the curator could introduce us.

The year before (1992) saw the publication of a book for children titled *Emily*. Written by Michael Bedard, this story book was a fictional tale about the relationship between Emily Dickinson and a little girl who lived in the house across the street. Cooney, who has published many books for children, including a book that won a Caldecott Award, was the illustrator.

I had heard that Cooney was going to place all of the original pictures for the book on long-term loan at the Jones Library. The curator had told me of his plans to exhibit the work upon receiving it. Yet I did not imagine that I would be there when Cooney and her daughter brought them, carrying them in her big artist's portfolio. Cooney was a petite woman with beautiful silver hair, which was braided and wound around her head. Her eyes were bright and shining. I enjoyed the pictures and her evocative explanations from her viewpoint as illustrator.

Picking up one drawing, she remarked, "Emily was dressed in white and of course needed an apron while gardening." In her illustration, she drew Emily in a blue apron. "The first illustration is the back of Emily at the door, and the last one is the same composition without Emily, but only the door with light coming in. This is to show Emily's freedom in spite of her so-called 'reclusive life.' I wanted to have a blank white page on the right-hand side of the last picture of the door. But the publisher printed the afterword there. Well, as you know, it is almost impossible to make a book just as one wants it."

She brought not only the pictures that had been printed in the book, but also her preliminary sketches and dummies. In one of her sketches, she drew Emily from the side, in profile. Since the only remaining photo left of Emily was taken from the front, I had always thought of her that way. I enjoyed this new portrayal of Emily created by Cooney's artistic sense.

Some readers think that Cooney took artistic license with The Homestead. It is red brick now, but it was painted ochre, according to the fashion of the period when Emily lived there. Even now, you can still see traces of yellow paint. In Cooney's illustration, The Homestead was correctly depicted as yellow, but she received so many letters from the readers protesting that the house should be red that she finally had to make pre-printed postcards in order to reply to them all.

For the opening of the exhibit, Cooney visited the library again for a book signing. The Special Collection section was filled with enthusiastic parents and children who were also touched by Cooney's Dickinson-inspired art. There were so many people waiting in line for her to sign books I felt that I did not want to join the queue and add to her work. But since she was greeting each person in line with so much enthusiasm I overcame my qualm. When my turn came, she recognized me and asked, "How's your project coming?" Then she inscribed my book with "Love to Masako." As she handed the book back to me she hesitated and opened it up again and said, "Oh, that's not enough." She added the inscription "Special Friend" and finally gave me back the book. Those words made me immensely happy but it was the graciousness and kindness that she showed to each individual in that long queue amidst a busy scene that touched me most.

When December was nearly at hand, I came across a notice in the local newspaper that Jane Langton was coming to a nearby bookshop for a reading and book signing to celebrate the publication of her new book, *Divine Inspiration*. Langton is also the author of a series of some ten mystery stories all set in New England. Her first mystery, *The Transcendental Murder*, is set in Concord, Massachusetts. Emerson, Hawthorne, and Thoreau are central characters. Dickinson plays a role as well — some of her poems are quoted and a fictitious love letter from Thoreau plays a part in the plot. Another one of her mysteries, *Emily Dickinson Is Dead*, is well-known among Dickinson fans. I took great pleasure in how Langton wove Dickinson elements into this fictitious tale.

On my way to the book signing I decided to have dinner in a restaurant near the bookstore. While I am accustomed to dining alone, I still I feel a little awkward, especially if it's a restaurant I've never been in before (which was the case here). Not having anything to read I cautiously scanned the other patrons in the dining room. The lady at the next table was also by herself. She had a look of elegance and dignity — silver hair, gray suit, black sweater and a white brooch. She seemed familiar. Then I remembered: She looked remarkably like the picture of Jane Langton in the newspaper. After I finished my dinner, I approached her and asked her if she were Jane Langton. She replied that she most certainly was, and since I was trying to be careful about not intruding too much on her privacy I bid her goodbye, mentioning that I was looking forward to seeing her at the bookstore.

As she signed each book, Langton also drew an accompanying illustration. Everyone there was so pleased and excited. When my turn came, since we had already "met" at the restaurant I plucked up the courage to ask her how she came up with the scene of a group of Japanese scholars at an international Dickinson conference that was depicted in *Emily Dickinson Is Dead.* "Oh, I'm afraid I might have been mean-spirited," she said. "That passage reinforces the stereotype of packs of Japanese dangling cameras from their necks. I'm ashamed I did that." As far as I know, there was only one Dickinson conference held before the novel was written and only one Japanese person attended, so Langton could not have found her inspiration there. Yet I acknowledged some truth in her description of Japanese tourists. I explained this, but she seemed embarrassed that I, as a Japanese woman, brought up the issue. She autographed my copy of *Dante Game,* a story set in Florence, and the Dante that she drew for me looked somewhat embarrassed. Every time I look at it, I regret having made her uncomfortable by asking the question — but, uncharacteristically, my curiosity had gotten the better of me.

(Another mystery writer, Joanne Dobson, used her expertise as a Dickinson scholar to craft a protagonist, Karen Pelletier, who is also a Dickinson scholar. In *Quieter Than Sleep,* Pelletier's knowledge of, and affinity for, Emily helps her solve the murders of her department chair and a student.)

One illustrator who does fascinating work is Christine Couture. I saw an announcement that she would host a walk to Amethyst Brook after her book signing. Some locals think that the brook's name inspired the phrase "an Amethyst remembrance" in Dickinson's poem "I held a Jewel in my fingers —" (J245). One of Couture's friends was a naturalist, who gave us information about what we saw on the way. When we got to the top of a peak, we beheld a gorgeous view and felt a nice, cool breeze on our cheeks.

Couture's first picture book was inspired by the house that had been my landlord's previous office. This prompted me to purchase her book *The House on the Hill,* in which the house is set upon a fictitious hill and nine children have adventures inside. The story and the characters are endearing. The house is now used partly as an office space for the Jeffrey Amherst Bookshop. Near the Jones Library and set back from the street, I hadn't noticed it before reading the book. Afterward, the dark gray building looked quite mysterious and alluring.

Couture and I became friends. She told me that she created pictures relating to Dickinson before, which had been out on loan. She invited me to the Allen House, where she was staying, so I could see them before they were to go out on loan again. The pictures were engaging and offered a more sophisticated perspective on Emily.

While at the Allen House I met Alan Zieminski and his brother, Jonas, who ran the inn. Jonas told me about a Dickinson play to be performed in sustain her performance as well as seamlessly blend what's true with what's imagined.

On another occasion, I saw a video of *The Belle of Amherst* in which Emily is played by the well-known British actress, Claire Bloom. It was recorded without an audience. Although some textual changes had been made, there were so many differences in Bloom's approach to the character of Emily that I was astonished that it was based on the same script. But I am open to different creative interpretations and enjoyed my encounter with this one. A Dickinson scholar told me that she had enjoyed Kim Hunter's *Belle* very much. Hunter came to Northampton during my stay in Amherst, not for *The Belle of Amherst*, but for *Love Letters*, which I enjoyed. I could see how she could be marvelous as Emily. Glenda Jackson, another British actress who has since retired to go into politics, also recorded Emily's poems. Her reading has something almost gruesome or dreadful about it — it lacks vulnerability. But, since her voice had such overwhelming power I appreciated hers as well.

When we arrived in Chatham, I phoned Harris. What answered at the other end of the line was *that voice* — the voice that I had associated so much with that of Emily's. While there was nothing strange about her voice per se, it was very strange to me to have a conversation with the voice that was Emily's. At a loss for words, I stammered an apology for the interruption and introduced myself. After a little bit of hesitation she remembered who I was. I asked whether she was going to appear in a play in the near future. She told me that she was going to appear in a play in New York in a few months. Another trip was in order so I could see her in this new play.

When I returned to Amherst, I called a friend of mine in New York. She invited me to stay with her and offered to see the play with me. I arrived at my friend's apartment just fifteen minutes before we needed to leave for the play. With no time at all to change into the kimono I brought, we dashed out. The play, *The Fiery Furnace*, written by Timothy Mason, was about a family in the Midwest in the 1950s and 1960s — a mother and her two daughters, all suffering at the hands of their husbands. I had read reviews of the play in *The New Yorker* and the *New York Times*. The latter featured a photo of Julie Harris along with the caption: "At 68, a Broadway Star Gets Ready to Make Her Off Broadway Debut." It would have been wonderful to have seen her in *The Belle of Amherst*. However, I enjoyed seeing her perform in something different. For Harris, Emily was not everything, although I came to know her through Emily.

*In Search of Emily*

I visited Irene Haas, a friend of mine who illustrates children's book, in New York. She introduced me to Will Barnet, a painter who was a friend of hers. I was familiar with his book of drawings based on Emily's poems. At the Mead Museum at Amherst College, I found one of his paintings among those representing contemporary American art. His works are characterized by clear, neat lines and a limited number of colors. When I see his paintings and react to his color palette I think of serenity and solitude. My friend also had a book of Barnet's collected works. His early works were characterized by vivid colors, half-abstract shapes, and children. I looked forward to seeing him in person.

Barnet lived in an apartment house exclusively for artists in Gramercy Park. A man was helping him put his oeuvre in order. Barnet, who appeared somewhat austere in the photo of him I had seen, was much more friendly and warm-hearted, although he was also a man of dignity, which the photos also revealed. He showed me a series of CDs made in Japan that featured his work on their covers. Barnet explained to me that the Japanese producer of the series asked permission to use the works since he liked them so much. The CDs had titles like "For pregnant women" and "For women at menopause." Barnet was amused when he heard me translate their titles.

We began to talk about Dickinson. Having spent two years reading and rereading her poems, Barnet made *The World in a Frame*, a book of illustrations based on her poems. He referred to it as a labor of love. He used special carbon pencils and period paper to create his black and white pictures. Barnet said, "Of course, I know that her dress should be white, even though it is black in my pictures." Usually somewhat picky about Dickinson details, I hadn't found that divergence strange in Barnet's work — perhaps because Emily's dress looks black in the only existing photo of her; or perhaps because I liked Barnet's drawing so much.

Various artists have created Emily's portraits based on this photo. Some of them represent her as rather frumpy and ugly. One of them made her look like an elephant. Other portraits of her are too beautiful: the one on a postage stamp is, according to Professor Porter, too much "like Audrey Hepburn." The front cover of Barnet's book is a drawing of Emily's face in full. I like this portrait very much because she is depicted with elegance and a touch of loveliness.

Barnet's drawings of Emily have an austerity and serenity. However, in one she is caught jumping, with her back to the viewer, "Inebriate of Air" —

a phrase from her poem, "I taste a liquor never brewed —" (J214) — celebrating her inebriation with nature. I was pleased to see the humorous side of Dickinson so vividly visualized. For "Wild Nights" (J249), he depicts Emily facing storms, both inside and outside.

I regretted the fact that I left my copy of his book back in Japan, so he could not autograph it. Generously, Barnet wrote his name and a dedication on a lithograph of Emily not included in the book. I said hesitantly, "After I came to know Emily, her spell has been so intense on me that no other poet can move me." Barnet replied, "I feel exactly the same way." We shook hands firmly as kindred spirits.

I presumed that the title of his book, *The World in a Frame*, was taken from a Dickinson poem. I consulted *A Concordance to the Poems of Emily Dickinson*. This alphabetically organized dictionary-sized book includes all of the occurrences of each word Dickinson used in her poems. Scholars have published concordances for most major writers. They are indispensable to understanding writers' semantic and linguistic tendencies. To compile a concordance used to be a tremendously arduous and tedious task but today computers have made it much easier. But searching through the concordance I could not find the phrase, neither under "world" nor "frame." I thought it might perhaps be a phrase from one of her letters. A concordance to her letters was not yet complete, so it would have been impossible to check every letter. I realized that I should have asked Barnet when I had the chance.

Back in Amherst, I accidentally ran into Christopher Benfey, who had published several books on Dickinson, including Barnet's. Benfey wrote the introduction to Barnet's book and I had audited his class on Whitman and Dickinson at Mount Holyoke College during my lengthy stay in 1986–87. We were waiting for the light to change so I took the opportunity to ask him about Barnet's book. "Oh, I made up the title for him," he said. "Really?" I replied, stunned. "It is so Emily-like that I was convinced it was her phrase." "Yes, it is Emily-like, isn't it?" He seemed flattered.

# The Evergreens

NEXT DOOR TO THE HOMESTEAD, ONLY 300 FEET AWAY, IS A PALE yellow two-story building. This house was Emily's brother, Austin's, residence — The Evergreens. When he learned of Austin's desire to go to the Midwest, their father, Edward Dickinson, provided him with the land and the house in 1855. It was an early wedding gift and an inducement for Austin to remain in Amherst. It worked. All five members of the Dickinson family lived out their lives in close proximity to each other. The Evergreens and its handsome outline can still be seen from The Homestead. Between the back doors of both houses runs a narrow path described by Emily as "just wide enough for two who love." This path was her link to The Evergreens.

The house was built in the Italian villa style, a romantic revival influence that originated in England and became popular in the United States in the 1840s. The style encompassed something between the spirit of a country house and the convenience of town life, and was characterized by an irregular floor plan with projecting balconies, verandahs, bays, and a tower set off by round-headed windows. The Evergreens was designed by William Fenno Pratt, a young architect from Northampton. The City Hall in Northampton was Pratt's first commission and helped to establish his reputation as an architect of note.

The Evergreens can be glimpsed from Main Street through a row of tall hemlocks and a lawn filled with shrubs and gardens, whose flowers and blossoms each season make a beautiful contrast with the creamy yellow of the house. Despite the appealing setting, there is something damp, gloomy, and cold about this house. Although The Homestead has been open to the public since 1965, the doors of The Evergreens had remained tightly shut and few people had been inside until recently.

After Austin's death in 1895, his widow, Susan Dickinson, spent eighteen years in the house. Their daughter, Martha Dickinson Bianchi, the only descendant, occupied the house for the next thirty years. Since she had been estranged from her husband, had no children, and her two brothers had both died young, she left the house to Alfred Leete Hampson, her secretary and editorial assistant. He married a mutual friend of theirs, Mary Landis, in 1947. After Alfred's death in 1952, Mary Hampson lived alone in the house for over thirty-five years, until she died in 1988 at the age of ninety-three. In her later years, as the literary recognition of Emily rose and interest in the Dickinson family increased, Mrs. Hampson was beset by scholars and strangers who were interested in getting a look inside the house. However, she invited only her closest friends and acquaintances into the house. So for over a hundred years the house has been handed down to only a few people, all closely related to each other. As a result, the furnishings and original atmosphere of the house were altered only slightly.

When I heard that Mrs. Hampson had died, I mourned her death, and I expected that The Evergreens would at last be open to the public. But this was only the beginning of a protracted battle that would determine whether the house should be preserved or demolished. Martha Dickinson Bianchi had included a clause in her will stating that "for sentimental reasons, I do not want my dwelling house to be occupied by anyone else." Fearing that the house might be converted into a fraternity residence or a business, she indicated that after the Hampsons no longer used it, the house was to be demolished — "taken down to the cellar." During the probate period, a friend in Amherst sent me newspaper articles about the debate on the house, which I read avidly, fearing that the worst might happen. The debate also brought to the forefront longstanding issues that the Dickinson family would rather have seen die. Dickinson Bianchi and Hampson both abhorred the possibility of further scandals related to the Dickinson family. It was quite natural for Dickinson Bianchi to hope to keep the details of her father's relationship with Mabel Todd, editor of Emily's poems, from the public eye. And she herself was not immune to scandal. She married Captain Alexander E. Bianchi in 1903, but he disappeared after spending time in jail on fraud charges. She filed for divorce and devoted her time to publishing her aunt's work with the assistance of Alfred Leete Hampson. Dickinson Bianchi and Hampson lived together at The Evergreens and traveled widely throughout Europe, which led to gossip among the residents of Amherst.

*The Path Between,* by Maravene S. Loeschke, is a novel based on Martha's life. According to the novel, in 1913 Dickinson Bianchi was alone, deserted by her husband. She found in Hampson a person who really understood her, her devotion to her family, and her literary talent. I once asked a Dickinson scholar, who was also an acquaintance of Mrs. Hampson's, how much of the story was true. His answer was, "Truth is stranger than fiction."

Whatever the truth might be, by the time I arrived in Amherst in 1993, the lawsuit was over and the Martha Dickinson Bianchi Trust had been charged by Hampson's will to "establish The Evergreens as a charitable and cultural facility for the enjoyment and/or cultural interest or fare of scholars and/or general public." Although not yet open, the house and its contents would eventually be, so I secretly hoped that there would be even a small chance for me to have a glance inside before I had to return to Japan. Only a very few Dickinson scholars in the United States or guides at The Homestead were lucky enough to gain entrance to The Evergreens; I feared I would leave the United States disappointed.

Soon after I arrived back, my landlord told me that his architecture firm was going to respond to a request for proposals for a feasibility study of The Evergreens. He added, "We may ask your opinion as a Dickinson scholar of international reputation." My being a Dickinson scholar "of international reputation" sounded quite inflated, so I paid little heed to what he had said.

Several weeks later, he told me that he had attended a meeting where he and other architects listened to a slide presentation on The Evergreens by Gregory Farmer, the project manager for the Martha Dickinson Bianchi Trust. Shortly thereafter he proposed that I join them at ten o'clock the day after next to see The Evergreens. I nearly jumped with joy.

The next day, I spoke with other architects at the firm who wanted to learn more about the background of the house. They also gave me more information on the project. Several architectural firms would present their proposals and one would be chosen to study the feasibility of restoring and reusing The Evergreens. A site visit at The Evergreens was scheduled as the only opportunity to inspect the property. I was to be one of the team members when they presented their proposal. I could not quite believe my luck and asked, "Why me? There are many American Dickinson scholars who could give you better advice. All I might do is to offer something of an outsider's view." They said, "That point of view is exactly what we need." I allowed myself to accept my good fortune. It looked like my enthusiasm was my main qualification.

The following morning we met at the architectural office and three of us headed toward The Evergreens. When we arrived, I found the door that had been tightly shut for so long now standing wide open. I stood there in utter amazement. There were already several architects inside the entrance hall. In front of me was a stairway leading up to the second floor and veering right at the landing halfway up. I felt that it would have been enough for me to remain there looking at the stairway, but I was to have the overwhelming joy of seeing much more of the house.

The entrance hall was decorated with red wallpaper and led to several other rooms. The window shades of each room were open, but the interior was dark. The wallpaper was peeling here and there, and there were piles of things on tables. The past seemed to have stopped breathing and to have stayed still in the house ever since.

After about fifteen of us gathered in the entry way and signed our names in a guest book. William Steelman, of Historic Massachusetts, Inc., and Gregory Farmer, of the Martha Dickinson Bianchi Trust, greeted us and gave us an introduction to the house. We were then free to look around inside. I had my camera with me, just in case, and by some miracle I was allowed to take pictures.

The first room on the right as you enter the house is the library, which served as Austin's law office after his downtown building burned in 1888. The bookcases were filled with books and the walls were hung with pictures with numbers assigned to them. Someone was evidently in the process of preparing an inventory and, when finished, it would provide useful information on what books Emily might have read and which pictures she might have seen. The material would be sure to contribute to a better understanding of her.

Austin was a collector of paintings. His main interest was the Hudson River School, the first generation of American landscape painters who recorded unspoiled natural settings. In recent studies of Emily, some scholars have reconsidered her place in the culture of the time. Austin's pictures have been taken into consideration as one of the sources of her poetic inspiration. Thus, it would be wonderful if scholars were able to have easier access to the paintings at The Evergreens, which so far have been admired by only a limited number of people. Many of the pictures had been removed for analysis and special conservation treatment. It was perhaps for inventorying purposes that there was a computer sitting on a table in the center of the room — a modern symbol making a sharp contrast with the antiquated atmosphere of the house.

The room behind the library is called "The Emily Room." I asked Farmer the reason and he explained that it had been used by Dickinson Bianchi in preparing her aunt's poems and letters for publication. Emily's furniture and belongings, inherited by her niece, had also been here. (Many of them were conveyed to Harvard University by Alfred Hampson through Gilbert Holland Montague in 1950–1951.) Originally, it had been the bedroom of Austin and his wife, but all evidence of that use was eliminated when the room was remodeled after Austin's death.

To the west of the hall, near the entrance, was a parlor. The first things that caught my eye upon entering were a mantelpiece and a large mirror and a white plaster cast of Antonio Canova's *Cupid and Psyche* (the original is in the Louvre). There were many books, paintings, and chairs, as well as a Steinway piano, which was Dickinson Bianchi's. This salon was the very room that saw assemblages many of the intellectual leaders of the nineteenth century. Among them was Ralph Waldo Emerson, who was invited to visit and stayed here when he lectured in Amherst on December 16, 1857. We wonder whether Emily might have come from next door to have a historic encounter with another one of the great minds of the time, but unfortunately no evidence of such a meeting survives. Although she was a poet, she was also totally unknown, and it seems to me that she may have eschewed meeting Emerson because he was "great." Her only reference to him — "It must have been as if he had come from where dreams are born" — is thought to have been uttered on this occasion. The parlor looked different from the historic picture with which I was familiar, which was taken during this time, although the room retained something of the appearance of the salon. Dickinson Bianchi used the room to entertain "pilgrims" who came to learn about her aunt, which may account for its more practical furnishings.

The next room was a dining room characterized by a lovely coffered oak ceiling, a gift to Austin from a Boston architectural firm in the 1880s. Under the chandelier in the center of the room was a solid square table and four chairs. Along the south wall were cabinets, a cupboard, and a Japanese-style screen. On the north side, a mantelpiece supported decorative tableware and another large mirror. In a corner behind a curtain was a small alcove fitted out as a pantry. The wallpaper in the dining room was blue with elaborate patterns.

Behind the dining room was a kitchen with a modern electric range and an old wood-burning cook stove. On the wall was another short row of books.

After viewing all the rooms on the first floor, I went upstairs. In each of the three main rooms on the second floor there were dusty boxes arrayed in a disorderly fashion on tables. Chairs were scattered here and there. There were many old books on the bookshelves and some new ones scattered around that had apparently belonged to Mary Hampson in her later years.

I surmised that Gib's room must be the one whose open door could be seen from the landing on the stairs. I had just finished reading *This Brief Tragedy* (the title taken from one of Emily's poems) by John Evangelist Walsh, published in 1991. His description of Gib's room had made a strong impression on me. Gib was the nickname of Thomas Gilbert Dickinson, the third child of Austin and his wife. On October 5, 1883, he died at the age of eight of typhoid fever. It was a great shock to all of the Dickinsons. Walsh suggests that this incident influenced Austin to pursue a deeper romantic relationship with Mabel Todd as a protest against fate. In addition, it may have made Emily give up plans to marry Judge Lord and publish her poetry. Walsh hypothesizes that the decline in her health was rooted in her collapse at this time.

In 1985, when he was in the midst of researching his book, Walsh came to Amherst with his wife and visited Mary Hampson. While his wife was having a chat with Hampson, Walsh made a surreptitious tour of the rooms and came to one room furtively. He had to give a push to open the door and found a tricycle, a rocking horse, and other children's toys inside. Walsh realized it was Gib's room and that the boy's mother Sue, sister Martha, and even the Hampsons might well have preferred to keep the room as it was. The room itself expressed the overwhelming impact of Gib's death on the people involved and convinced Walsh of his theory.

I thought I was ready to see the room, yet I paused in front of the door, almost afraid to touch it. The other people did not seem to have a special interest in this room. The hallway was very still and I was the only one there. Upon entering the room, I could immediately sense it was a nursery. The room was filled with all manner of things — as if Gib were to return at any moment. I saw an old iron tricycle, and a wooden rocking horse waiting expectantly for a rider. On the wall was a print of a child praying piously, his head bowed and hands clasped. As I looked about, it pained me to see the clippings pasted to the closet door — childhood visions of animals and children. The images had turned yellow with age and each picture had been neatly placed on the closet door, with another set of pictures on the back of the door leading to the hall. Did Gib imitate his father's collection of paintings and make a child's version?

Gib was a child possessed with great sensitivity. For example, Gib could not bear to see even the pictures of one of his little friends who had left town. Dickinson Bianchi recorded some episodes of Gib's life in her book, *Emily Dickinson: Face to Face*. Once, when he was stung on the arm by a wasp, he begged his mother through his tears to read the Bible to the wasps. On another occasion when she tried to teach him to sing "There's No Place Like Home," he broke in, "Yes, there is too! Over at Aunt Emily's! Over at Aunt Emily's!" The following Dickinson poem is surmised to have been sent to Gib:

> Not at Home to Callers
> Says the Naked Tree —
> Bonnet due in April —
> Wishing you Good Day —   (J1590)

Gib's charms were noted not only by his aunt, but also by the age of eight he was already something of an idol in town, beloved by all. The *Amherst Record*, the town's weekly newspaper, ran his obituary in which the writer noted the broad and intense affection for him. The tribute ends with this sentence: "He not only promised much, but he already had provided much." It was quite unusual for a young child to have such a long obituary and it read as if it were describing an adult, testimony to his uniqueness. Two photographs, taken shortly before his illness show Gib with long hair and a childish sweetness mixed with thoughtful melancholy.

Gib's room has a window cut into an interior wall next to the hall door, so that someone passing through the hall could look in on the child without disturbing him. The nursery has a brass bed, but I was told that Gib died in the first floor bedroom, the reason why the lower bedroom has traditionally been known as "the dying room."

A friend and neighbor wrote in a letter to her son about the effect of Gib's illness on Emily: "the odor from the disinfectants used, sickened her so that she was obliged to go home . . . and vomited." As a result, she was in bed for several weeks. Emily herself wrote, "The Physician says I have 'Nervous prostration.'" After this ordeal, she never quite recovered, physically or mentally. As for Austin, it was said that his sister, Lavinia, had to work hard to keep him from following Gib to the grave.

Emily sent several letters of sympathy to her sister-in-law and wrote four poems about Gib's death, including the following:

> Pass to thy rendezvous of Light,
> Pangless except for us —
> Who slowly ford the Mystery
> Which thou hast leaped across!    (J1564)

Toward the end of the year, she confided in Mrs. Holland, one of her best friends:

"Open the Door, open the Door, they are waiting for me," was Gilbert's sweet command in delirium. *Who* were waiting for him, all we possess we would give to know — Anguish at last opened it, and he ran to the little Grave at his Grandparents' feet — All this and more, though is there more? More than Love and Death? Then tell me it's name!    (L873)

Three of the extant Christmas greetings of that year are filled with sorrowful words, like "Santa Clause comes with a Smile and a Tear."

Deep in thought about Gib, I was about to leave the room when I heard a fly and one of Emily's poems came to my mind:

> I heard a Fly buzz — when I died —
> The Stillness in the Room
> Was like the Stillness in the Air —
> Between the Heaves of Storm —
>
> The Eyes around — had wrung them dry —
> And Breaths were gathering firm
> For that last Onset — when the King
> Be witnessed — in the Room —

> I willed my Keepsakes — Signed away
> What portion of me be
> Assignable — and then it was
> There interposed a Fly —
>
> With Blue — uncertain stumbling Buzz —
> Between the light — and me —
> And then the Windows failed — and then
> I could not see to see —     (J465)

    I continued down the hall. Passing a maid's room, I came to a narrow stairway leading to the kitchen. The stairway turned and continued down another flight to the cellar, which was very spacious. In strong contrast to the disordered clutter of the other rooms, the cellar was practically bare. It was so damp down there that Hampson had to have things taken out. In one corner were portions of the old fence and gate posts, which had collapsed a few years earlier. Old pictures of The Evergreens showed how the fence had complemented the house.

    Ascending from the cellar, I still had one more place to examine — the tower, a small square room raised above the second floor in a manner characteristic of the Italian villa style. The Homestead had a similar element, a cupola, attached at about the same period by Pratt, the architect for The Evergreens. Neither the tower nor the cupola were furnished since they were primarily thought to be for ventilation. The stairway to the tower of The Evergreens was very narrow and fit just one person. The tower room itself had pairs of tall wood-framed windows looking out on each of the four directions. The floor, covered with woven straw matting, was stacked with piles of old magazines tied up with string. I bent down to examine one of them and found Edward Dickinson's name in pencil, and the date — 1830! I looked again carefully — it was 1830, the year in which Emily was born. I pondered, with wonder, my relationship to her, from such a distant place and time. Because of her, I was exploring this great house. I would not have been surprised if she herself appeared in this house where time seemed to have stopped for over a hundred years. I was suddenly struck by the extraordinary infinity and mystery of time, and Emily's words surfaced: "I find ecstasy in living — the mere sense of living is joy enough" (L342a).

    I stood up and peeked out a window. The foliage on the trees was green and full, and the New England wind was cool and fresh. All the sorrows I had ever experienced so far seemed to have been endured so I could experience this moment. And every joy I've ever experienced led me to this moment too — that this moment surpassed any joy I had ever experienced. I cherished this moment, for I knew in the next all of the sorrows and joys of my life would come rushing back. I shed some silent tears:

> This quiet Dust was Gentlemen and Ladies
> And Lads and Girls —
> Was laughter and ability and Sighing
> And Frocks and Curls.
>
> This Passive Place a Summer's nimble mansion
> Where Bloom and Bees
> Exists an Oriental Circuit
> Then cease, like these —     (J813)

This poem, about the evanescence of this life with its "dust to dust" image, is also about death. The "dust" could be interpreted literally, like the layer on everything in this old house. And in the quiet dust, what drama.

The Evergreens would eventually be restored and opened to the public. I was lucky enough to have had a chance to see it in its disorder and dinginess, somehow sadly suitable for a house that has weathered so much.

After our team had submitted our proposal for the re-use feasibility study of The Evergreens, we learned that our proposal was among the final three. We were to be interviewed. The five of us — two architects, a marketing consultant, me, and another historical and literary advisor — met Steelman and Farmer in the dining room of The Evergreens. After the interview, we looked again through the rooms. Fearing that this might be the last time for me to see the house until its opening to the public, I dared ask if I might play the piano in the parlor. "I'm afraid it is out of tune," Farmer said. It was exactly what I wanted, the music that would come from it would fit the present dilapidated condition of this sad house where time seemed to stand still. So I played Chopin's "Farewell Waltz," which sounded even more melancholy and sentimental being played off-key. Afterward, Farmer showed us pictures of Dickinson Bianchi and her husband, Captain Bianchi, which I had never seen before.

It was the end of June when we heard they had chosen our team for the restoration project. I was filled with joy, excitement, and gratitude. And I was thrilled at the prospect of being more deeply involved with The Evergreens and to have the invaluable experience of closely seeing how this kind of restoration was done in the United States. Several months later, we presented a report as thick as a book. It described The Evergreens today, provided a market study, and proposed how it should be run when opened as a historic house. A full budget for the restoration and re-use of the building rounded out the report.

During the process of drawing up this report I had been recording my experiences and writing about The Evergreens. I dared to ask Farmer to check my facts for accuracy. He was happy to do it. A few days later, he returned my pages with a note saying, "I like it. You've caught the sentiment of the house." He had corrected my mistakes and added new information that I had missed. I was truly appreciative. Then, a few weeks later, Farmer told me, "I was asked to write about The Evergreens for the *Massachusetts Review*. I told them, 'There's already a piece ready for you.' And I recommended yours." I was surprised and honored by this.

When the article came out, my somewhat sentimental description of The Evergreens and Farmer's objective one were matched with some pictures by photographer Jerome Liebling. His photos were marvelous, the work of a true artist. He captured items in the house from viewpoints amateurs might easily have missed. There were close ups of the rocking horse and a collection of shoes that appeared to have belonged to the children. His photos were marked by elegance and deep sensitivity. It was also great to get to know Liebling with his warm, generous personality. The photo of shoes was featured on the cover of the *Massachusetts Review* and I was happy and proud to see it whenever I went to bookshops in Amherst that winter.

# A Dancing Star

DANIEL LOMBARDO, THE CURATOR OF THE DICKINSON, FROST AND Francis collections at the Jones Library, was sorry that he had missed the chance to see me when I wore my *kimono* when I gave a presentation to the guides at The Homestead. He said half jokingly, "Why don't you read Emily's poetry here in the library in your kimono?" I think that he might have surmised that I wanted to give a reading again, since I had had one there seven years earlier. At that time, having given several Dickinson poetry readings with a reader in Japan, I thought it worthwhile to offer something similar in Amherst in English. However, I did not want to do the same thing I did there the last time — mere repetition would not yield greater depth. Thus, without any overwhelming desire to organize a reading, I accepted Lombardo's invitation half jokingly on my part. In order to present a poetry reading with a different perspective, I had to find a reader who knew Dickinson's work and life very well, and who was also willing to work with me.

During this visit to Amherst in 1993, Wendy Kohler, one of the three organizers of the Summer Institute for Dickinson, held a reunion for seven of us (and some of their family members) who attended the institute in 1990. We all met at her house. One of them was Deborah Floyd, who was not only a teacher but also an actress. Three years before, during our institute, she had acted the role of heroine in the play *Another Part of the Forest*, which we had enjoyed. She was very pretty, but that was not her only virtue. Whenever I saw her, I felt as if the essence of her life itself were sparkling. That was what I liked best about her. Now she was a mother of a nearly one-year-old baby. I asked whether I would have another chance to see her on stage and she replied, "Well, you see, I have Emma now." Then I said, "I know it is difficult to take time for rehearsals and everything, but, for example, in case of a poetry reading . . ." So saying, I realized that she was exactly the person for whom I had been looking. "That is exactly what I'd like to do," she enthused on hearing my plan.

When we first got together to discuss what we wanted to do, Floyd said, "I wrote my master's thesis on Emily. I could continue to pursue the same track for my doctoral degree but I could not continue to focus on her as the object of my study. That's why I am a doctoral student in the educational field now. I like my job of teaching also. I admire your courage to pursue the path of a Dickinson scholar."

On hearing this, my heart was filled with joy to have found a congenial spirit. "What you feel toward Emily is exactly what I feel. I also find it hard to 'study' her. I tried to avoid it, but finally I found I have to be a Dickinson scholar. But I can never be a good one because I simply like her too much. What I want to do is to help people enjoy her much more. For example, something like this poetry reading is exactly what I want to do but I don't speak well and I need someone to read. See? You know how happy I am to work with you."

It was a delight to create a program with her. I always felt special pleasure in working with someone who is truly competent and professional. First, we racked our brains to select a theme for the reading. Floyd showed what she had written on the first page of her copy of *The Collected Poems of Emily Dickinson* — it was a quotation from Nietzsche: "You must have chaos within you to give birth to a dancing star." "What a coincidence," I replied. "I bought a framed work of that same exact quote in a store in downtown Amherst."

That is how we settled on "A Dancing Star" as the title for the reading. The next step was to divide the program into three parts: Religious Chaos, Love Chaos and Poetic Chaos. We chose poems for each part, which was again a delightful process. We examined poems each of us had picked. Floyd read one aloud and said, "What a wonderful poem!" with insuppressible admiration. I felt all over again the happiness of working with someone who loved Emily with the same zeal I have. Her reading was suffused with the essence of her charm.

I woke up one night with a nightmare and found myself trembling with fear. I could not exactly remember what the dream was about, but I had the distinct sense of falling down endlessly into an abyss. I was overwhelmed by the notion that a human being must be born alone and die alone, something I try not to think about in daily life, to avoid this bottomless fear. On that night, I felt as if I were the only human being in the whole universe. The vividness of that feeling stayed with me. I turned to Emily and her poems seemed to speak about the same experience:

> Departed — to the Judgment —
> A Mighty Afternoon —
> Great Clouds — like Ushers — leaning —
> Creation — looking on —
>
> The Flesh — Surrendered — Cancelled —
> The Bodiless — begun —
> Two Worlds — like Audiences — disperse —
> And leave the Soul — alone —    (J524)

While "Judgment" is a Western and a Christian concept, the solitude in this vast world is common to everyone. Emily faced it in her attempt to verbalize it. I talked about this to Floyd at one of our meetings. She said, "I have had the same kind of experience. I wake up at night and fear seizes me. My husband's there but even that does not help. Even now that I have Emma that sense of aloneness can never be erased." I was glad she understood me immediately. I had talked about this with some of my friends, who consoled me saying it might have something to do with the fact that I was alone in a foreign country or that I am unmarried. So I had to explain, "No, the issue is completely different. It is an existential one that can never be shaken as long as one is alive."

Emily, in a well-known poem beginning "I felt a Funeral, in my Brain," expressed the sense of falling in this way in the poem's last stanza:

> And then a Plank in Reason, broke,
> And I dropped down, and down —
> And hit a World, at every plunge,
> And Finished knowing — then —   (J280)

When I read this poem for the first time during my university days, I was surprised at the exacting visualization of the ghastly scene, a depiction that was drawn so sharply in only few words. I wondered who else could have written something like this. With that in mind, we chose to include the former poem (J524) in our program.

Floyd had a packed schedule being Emma's mother, a teacher, and a doctoral student. And I was busy, too. So when we met to discuss the program, we had to work efficiently, having no time to waste. We had about ten meetings and each time I sensed that we made steady progress toward crafting the final performance. I always have to face stage fright when I am in front of people, but this time I was eager for the day to come, since the performance would be the culmination of all we had done so far. A stage actor or actress will reveal something that cannot be found at any rehearsal once s/he has an audience. My role was to speak about Emily and her poetry. I would do my best so that Floyd could emit her brightest sparks.

In order to make this poetry reading possible, Lombardo's help was indispensable. He prepared the setting at the library. His assistant, Marty Noblick, made the programs. The day before we had a dress rehearsal at the reading room of the Special Collections department with Lombardo as an audience. I began with a brief talk on my translations, and read some examples. Some readings in Japanese were included in the program to provide the audience with a chance to listen to the sound of the Japanese translations. I believe one should have a good voice, training, and nerve in order to read on stage. That's why it is my rule to never read. But this was an emergency case. I did not have a Japanese reader available to read for me in Amherst. Still, I suffered the pangs of conscience on breaking my own rule. To my delight, Lombardo liked our reading very much. He liked the idea of our dual approach to Emily— mine from presenting her in a totally different culture and in Floyd's case from portraying Emily as a contemporary. She claimed that "I'm not going to be Emily. I want to present what it's like to read Emily now, in the year 1993." She was pleased that Lombardo caught the essence of her reading.

With a successful dress rehearsal, we were ready for the next day's performance, which was the night before Emily's birthday, December 10. When the lights came on, Floyd of course showed her best. Each word she spoke was alive. We had a full house. In the library there was a huge portrait of Emily, who we felt was also listening to us.

# The Ever-Changing World of Emily

AFTER MY SECOND EXTENDED STAY IN 1993–1994, I RETURNED TO Amherst often for brief visits that allowed me to witness many changes that had taken place in Emily's world. In 1996, The Homestead got a new curator, Cynthia Dickinson. Although she always introduces herself as "no relation," it's an amazing coincidence to meet another Dickinson there. Previously, curators were always from the staff of Amherst College. To fill the vacancy this time they advertised for the post. Cindy Dickinson's interests were not necessarily focused on Emily, but rather on literary history, museums, and historic preservation. Her impressive background provided a different perspective on how to manage The Homestead. Among other innovations, she opened more rooms to visitors.

One of her great projects was a new Dickinson dress replica. The original cotton dress holds a special place in the hearts of Dickinson fans. The Amherst Historical Society, which owns the dress, and The Homestead, finding its preservation long overdue, agreed to preserve it for the future. A costume maker and preservationist created a pattern from the original dress and a firm that specialized in historic textile reproduction recreated the fabric. The cost of the two replicas was approximately $10,000.

The annual meeting of Emily Dickinson International Society was held in Amherst in late spring in 1997. One of the main events was an exhibition titled "Language as Object: Emily Dickinson and Contemporary Art" at Amherst College's Mead Art Museum. It included works by well-established artists, like Joseph Cornell's boxes, Judy Chicago's "Emily Dickinson Plate," and Will Barnet's paintings. It also included pieces by young artists working in a variety of styles, from representational to abstract. Videos were constantly running. Among other things, there was a sculpture of Emily's white dress with letters carved in it and a small model of a staircase. In the room named "The Emily Dickinson Reading Room," her dress, the daguerreotype, and numerous popular culture images of the poet were on display. I was especially happy that work done by one of my friends — Barbara Penn — was included in the show. The exhibition was the result of three years of preparation by Susan Danly, its curator. It ended its two-month run on the last day of the society's meeting. It was stunning to see the power of the assemblage, to see in one space how much and how diversely Emily influenced others.

In conjunction with this exhibit, the Sleeveless Theatre's "Emily Unplugged," a new play by a local theater group, was presented at Amherst College's Kirby Theater to kick off the annual meeting. A one-woman play like *The Belle of Amherst*, this concept was completely different. As the program explained, this play was "a comic look at Dickinson in the context of today's Amherst." The play owed much of its success to the actress K.D. Halpin, who smoothly and hilariously transformed from one persona to another — Emily herself auditioning for the part of herself in the play, Emily as a rock star and many others. The audience applauded and cheered enthusiastically when Emily corrected Mabel Todd's version of one of her poems on a chalkboard.

During an informal luncheon session at the annual meeting, Daniel Lombardo, curator of Special Collections at the Jones Library, announced the upcoming sale of an unpublished Dickinson poem, of which he had been informed by Sotheby's. There was an overwhelming air of excitement in the room. When I read a copy of the poem, my initial impression was that it lacked the enigmatic aspect characteristic of so many of Emily's poems. Yet, there was a possibility that this particular poem had been written for the children of the family, since two words, "Aunt Emily," were inscribed on the back. The annual meeting attendees wanted to help bring the manuscript "back" to Amherst. With the money the society members pledged within an incredible short period of time, the library's budget, and funds from the Friends of the Jones Library, a few days later Lombardo succeeded in bidding $21,000 on the poem.

But before bidding on the poem, Lombardo had contacted Ralph Franklin, the editor of *The Manuscript Books of Emily Dickinson*, to get his opinion on its authenticity. Franklin, who knew Dickinson's handwriting better than anyone, did not find reason to doubt that the paper and the characteristics of the handwriting were inauthentic. In fact, Franklin wanted to include the poem in a variorum edition of Dickinson's poems that he was compiling for Harvard University Press. So Lombardo went ahead and secured the poem manuscript. About a month later Franklin informed Lombardo that he received a phone call from someone who claimed the poem was once in the hands of Mark Hofmann, a dealer who sold both authentic and fake manuscripts. Thus, the issue of authenticity became a more important part of the picture. But the issue as to its authenticity was still not completely resolved. As the history of the whereabouts of the poem was revealed, its authenticity became more and more suspect. Eventually with the help of science — ultraviolet light and a stereo-microscope — the two sleuths, Lombardo and Franklin, came to the conclusion that the piece was a forgery.

A few months later, I received a letter and my returned check from the Jones Library. The manuscript had proven fake after all. Sotheby's returned the money and the library was returning funds to those who generously donated them to acquire the manuscript. It was sad to hear about all this, and also very strange. Hofmann was one of the most notorious forgers of the twentieth century. He had been sentenced to life in prison for two pipe-bomb murders. It took a near-genius to make a forgery that might deceive an authority like Franklin.

Dickinson scholars had been hearing for some time of Franklin's plans to publish a new complete set of her poems. Finally, 1998 saw the publication of *The Poems of Emily Dickinson* in three volumes. The main differences from the Johnson edition are a revised chronology with more accurate dating of poems and a new numbering system. The total number of poems in his edition is 1,789 not because new poems were found, but because of new arrangements. In some cases, poems were combined; in other cases, separated. Editing Dickinson is truly a daunting job since it is impossible to know in what format, if any, she wanted to be published. Thus, Franklin's variorum is surely the best form in which we can hope to see her work. It is a major achievement in Dickinson studies.

It is interesting and intriguing to study the history of the publication of Emily's poems. Early on, some of her original words were changed without her permission or the readers' knowledge. Now readers can see the poems exactly as she wrote them. Thus, she raises fundamental questions: What is poetry? What is editing? What is it to be a poet and what is it to be a reader, and what is the relationship between the two? Who decides what the text of the poem should be?

What is on the printed page is something static — it gives an impression that a poem is finished and completed. But what concerned Emily most was that her verse "was alive" or "breathed." The fact that she left so many variants perhaps shows that she wanted to keep her work always unfinished, in progress. She wanted always to be at work, to be revising continually. Verse, for her, was not something static; rather, it was dynamic.

Another reason why I still wait for all her poems to appear in facsimile form is that she left many poems on pieces of paper of various forms — on the back of the envelope of a letter she received, or a chocolate wrapper. In one example, the piece is really oblong like a ruler. One scholar claims, for example, that a sheet on which a bird poem is written was cut in a bird shape. Are these instances simply the result of when proper paper was not near at hand or did Emily deliberately choose or form the shape of the paper? There are other examples when she made some clippings of pictures from printed pages and combined them with her poems. Does this serve as proof that she was conscious of how to present her work? These views have been addressed in critical papers and books. In many cases, we have to see the originals, which are kept in several places. A variorum facsimile will give us immense satisfaction and encourage us to further pursue investigation of Emily's mysteries.

The facsimile edition has been partially realized, thanks to developments in electronic technology. In 1996, the *Dickinson Electronic Archives* were begun. The website <http://www.emilydickinson.org> is devoted to the study of Dickinson, her writing practices, writings generated by her work, and writings of others that directly influenced her work. It was created by the Dickinson Editing Collective, and is supervised by four general editors, Martha Nell Smith, Ellen Louise Hart, Marta Werner, and Lara Vetter. The collective believes that "print translation of her work erases most of

Dickinson's visual poetics." They hope to "show the writer at work; i.e., to display the handwritten records of her composing habits."

In addition to gaining a new curator (now the director) at The Homestead, the Special Collections at the Jones Library gained a new curator. I miss the previous curator, Daniel Lombardo, very much, for going back to Amherst and to the Special Collections room in the Jones Library to work meant seeing Lombardo as well. But he is now available to act as my consulting editor during his free time, and I can't think of anyone better for that task.

A few days after arriving in the United States in February 2000, I found an announcement in the *New York Times* about a performance of "My Business Is to Love: Emily Dickinson in Words and Music" by Renee Fleming and Julie Harris. "My business is to love" is found in a Dickinson letter (L269) and is one of her key phrases along with "My Business is Circumference" (L268) and "My business is to sing" (L269). I was disappointed that I would not be able to travel to New York to attend the performance. I had to satisfy myself with reading the reviews in the *New York Times* a few days later and in the May/June issue of Emily Dickinson International Society's *Bulletin*.

In this performance, Harris performed an abridged version of *The Belle of Amherst*. This adaptation was a narrative that, between the readings, included performances of songs set to Dickinson texts. Nine composers were represented, and some pieces were premieres. Aaron Copland's work was included. His compositions, titled "Twelve Poems of Emily Dickinson" (piano version) and "Eight Poems of Emily Dickinson" (orchestra version) are some of the best-known music composed for Emily's work.

I decided to write Harris to ask for a recording of the performance and also find out about her stage schedule during my stay. I found out that in September she would go on the road again with *The Belle of Amherst* for about six months. She would be back in the legendary role to the delight of old fans, as well as a new generation of younger people. In a letter she added, "I'm going to send you a book that perhaps you're not familiar with." I was utterly curious about what book it might be. In a few weeks a package arrived — in it was one of the Penguin classics written by Thomas W. Higginson titled *Army Life in a Black Regiment and Other Writings*. I did not know that his work had been included in the Penguin series. Other Dickinson scholars with whom I shared the news had not known that, either. I shared the story with Professor David Porter, professor emeritus at UMass, who in a way had introduced me to Harris. He was very much impressed by her commitment as an actress, not only to play a role but also to maintain a broad interest in the character she played. And, there seemed to be a resurgence of Higginson's work. I found two thick books published in 2000: *The Magnificent Activist: The Writings of Thomas Wentworth Higginson* and Higginson's *The Complete Civil War Journal and Selected Letters*.

As happy as I was to renew my correspondence with Harris, I also had to face a piece of sad news. In early March, I found an obituary in the *New York Times* for Barbara Cooney, illustrator of the children's book, *Emily*. She was 83, and the photo of her in the newspaper captured her brilliant gray hair in braids, and her smile. The article quoted her: "How many children will realize that every flower and grass in the book grew in Chaucer's time in England? How many children will know or care? . . . Yet if I put enough in my pictures, there may be something for everyone. Not all will be understood, but some will be understood now and maybe more later." Several days later, I saw her original pictures for *Emily*, on loan to the Jones Library, being packed to be returned. I was saddened, thinking about my brief encounter with her at the Jones Library.

On arriving again in the United States, I was immediately absorbed in America's enthusiasm for Emily. The assistant for the Special Collections at the Jones Library was apparently waiting impatiently for me to arrive. She said, "I have something very interesting to show you," and led me to her computer. On the screen was a photo of a middle-aged woman. "This is supposed to be Emily Dickinson as an adult. What do you think?" It is widely believed that there is only one photograph of Emily, a daguerreotype taken in her mid-teens. As a result, her appearance as an adult has been largely unknown. After my first shock and surprise subsided, I learned more about the photo's circumstances.

In the middle of April, Professor Philip Gura of the University of North Carolina bought an album imprinted with the name Emily Dickinson written on the back. He set up a web site to solicit an open discussion, claiming that there were uncanny resemblances between this image and her daguerreotype. He was also careful to question its authenticity. There was research to be done: analyses of the facial structures in the two pictures, the handwriting in the inscription, and the chair in the photo with its unique characteristics. I noticed that the daguerreotype pictured a younger Emily with an expression of uneasy adolescence. This new find showed a woman with a self-composed, almost determined look. The more I looked at the photo, the more I wavered. Whatever the truth may be, it is quite like Emily to confuse and bewitch us with her mysteries.

There are always new discoveries concerning Emily Dickinson. In the middle of June 2000, the local newspaper reported that Amherst College purchased from a private dealer a Latin textbook that Emily and her friend Abiah Root shared as students at Amherst Academy. What is most valuable about the new acquisition is that it has Emily's handwritten notes, which were examined by Ralph Franklin, a specialist in her handwriting. Nearly every page has some marginalia, which shows how thoroughly Latin education was undertaken during that time. Yet, the classes must also have been somewhat tiresome — the two girls scribbled complaints about the homework, or doodled, adding decorations around the line numbers. The book, which also had a note from Emily that read "When I am far, far then think of me — E. Dickinson," ended up in Root's possession. Other notes included English translations of Virgil, one from Robert Browning. A scholar who saw the book as early as 1986 recorded that one of the footnotes referred to the color white: "This is an emblem of divinity; white being the color assigned to the celestial gods." To connect this with Emily's "White election" (J528) may be far-fetched, yet it is enticing. When I was allowed to see the book in the Frost Library, I needed only to flip through a few pages before I encountered almost ten pressed flowers and a short piece of hair, which was red and seemed "bold as a chestnut bur."

Later that month, I found, among other theatrical performances in a local newspaper listing of cultural events, an entry for *Emily*, "a new play about Emily Dickinson" to be presented by Mixed Company and Out-of-Town Productions. Juliana Dupre, a guide emeritus at The Homestead, graciously agreed to make the hour-long trip to the Berkshire town of Great Barrington with me. The theater was small and there were only about twenty people in the audience; yet it was not necessarily a poor showing, considering the show's nearly month-long run. And above all, the small size of the performance space was, it seemed to me, exactly what the play called for; in the playbill, the playwright, Mickey Freidman, contrasted Emily's "limited physical space" with the "extraordinarily large universe." He went on to explain that the play "is about Emily's unique soul-space: a place where physical history meets the life of the imagination." The most conspicuous thing about this new play was that there were two Emilys — "Young Emily" and "Emily." They were not intended to personify her, but rather act as presentations of her psychological world. The actress who played the part of "Young

Emily" was a college student, and her baby-faced youth worked well in contrast to the mature actress playing "Emily." Their similarities and differences produced an atmosphere of tension, somewhat like the anxiety Emily must have felt toward her own existence.

The year 2000 also saw an important Dickinson publication — *The Concordance to the Letters of Emily Dickinson*. It had been eagerly anticipated by Dickinson scholars and fans who had heard that this work was in progress. The letters are integral to understanding Dickinson. Without a concordance to the letters, it was difficult to have a complete image of her vocabulary. The concordance lists all of the words in her letters alphabetically and they are arranged with their contexts and frequencies. Used along with the concordance to the poems, it is a great help in making new discoveries. A year before, at the International Dickinson Conference at Mount Holyoke College, I had a chance to talk personally with the editor, Cynthia MacKenzie. She said, "When I entered the last letter in my computer, tears welled up in my eyes." That last letter is the commonly referred to as the "Called Back" letter, which consists of just those two words.

Although my stay in Amherst was relatively short this time, I quickly and easily caught up on Dickinson-related events and activities. As soon as I arrived, I was asked to join the Amherst-Kanegasaki sister city committee. It was a great opportunity for me to do something to better the understanding between the two towns, and the two countries. Once or twice a month we had meetings at Town Hall. The major issue was what we could do to receive Kanegasaki Junior High School students who were coming to visit Amherst for about a week. Unfortunately, I was going to be in California during their visit and it was a pity that it would be impossible for me to serve as their guide at The Homestead. We decided to make a brochure for them instead. I thought, why not also include Frost as well as another Amherst resident, William Clark, whose words, "Boys, be ambitious" are so well known in Japan? Clark helped found the Massachusetts Agricultural College (now UMass) and Sapporo Agricultural College (now the University of Hokkaido). The brochure would make a nice little souvenir. I wrote the materials on Dickinson and Frost, then translated what Ruth Jones, another member of the committee and history writer, wrote on Clark. I wanted to include a few Dickinson poems in the limited space. To my surprise and consternation, I found it rather difficult to choose among them. I hoped the students would immediately be caught by Emily's charm, although I knew that was optimistic. Given the need for more background for the translations and the cultural issues, just presenting the poems would not be enough.

The selection led me to think more about it, and to write a paper on presenting Dickinson to children. I compared American children's enthusiasm to the difficulty of presenting her to Japanese children. When, toward the end of my stay, I was asked to give a talk to the guides at The Homestead, I chose this topic as a theme. I hoped to learn from their experiences with children as well. After the Japanese students' visit, I decided to make a set of brochures for adults, and worked to get permission to include poems by Dickinson and Frost. These brochures turned out to be useful since the town of Kanegasaki later sent a delegation of adults to visit Amherst.

Every year, I receive appeals for the support of The Homestead and The Evergreens. Through many tours of the former home, and the opportunity to work on the team that assessed the feasibility of the latter's preservation and re-use, the future of both houses is often on my mind. I conceived of an idea to combine my love of Emily with my sister's love of music by having a fundraising concert for the houses. Gregory Farmer, project manager of The Evergreens, agreed to the idea and suggested that the First Congregational Church, just in front of The Evergreens, be the concert's location. As Dickinson's brother, Austin, had been involved in the church's construction, and several other members of the family had been members, it was a perfect place for the concert. Tour guides at The Homestead helped with the publicity. My sister, Makiko, a concert pianist, came from Germany, as did eight members of her Japanese fan club, and another from England, for the June 13th concert, making it a truly international event. Many of my Amherst friends later told me how impressed they were by my sister's performance. After the concert, Farmer had an open house at The Evergreens. Candles were lit around the porch and the light shone through the rain.

The annual "Poetry Walk" to commemorate the anniversary of Emily's death drew a large crowd in 2000. We began the walk by visiting several Dickinson-related spots and held poetry readings at each. At the end, as usual, people gathered at her gravestone to read a poem or two they had chosen. The director of The Homestead had asked me to join in the reading, and I brought "To make a prairie" (J1755) because it was the first Dickinson poem I had ever encountered and because it was so brief. I also read my own Japanese translation. On this day, there was a crew of people making a documentary film on Dickinson and I found myself being filmed. After the event, several people were asked to remain for more shots. I was asked to recite other poems and translations. As nervous as I was, I appreciated this rare chance to play a part in telling people about Dickinson from a different, Japanese, point of view. (Unfortunately, the Poetry Walk segment never made the final cut in the documentary.)

A similar opportunity presented itself later that day. Cindy Dickinson, the director of The Homestead, suggested I go with her to ACTV (Amherst Cable Television), the local cable access station, to talk about Emily for a program called *Age Is the Rage*. Since I didn't get much notice I didn't have time to worry about my casual dress. It was an interview program that usually focused on the lives and opinions of senior citizens. However, for this show they invited people who were interested in Dickinson. When we arrived at the studio, we found Sean Vernon, a singer, writer, and teacher who had set Emily's poems to music, just finishing his interview. I was asked about my first impression of The Homestead, the difficulty of translating Emily's poetry, and more. Although I experienced a bit of stage fright, it was an honor to have the experience for Emily's sake. Weeks later, I had a chance to see the show. Although I chided myself whenever I heard my English mistakes, I enjoyed watching it. The director of The Homestead said, "Not bad, huh?" I do hope so.

Every summer an organization in Japan arranges for a group to visit The Homestead. The director of The Homestead asked me to be their guide. I was honored and agreed. She lent me a guide manual for a few days, and I experienced a feeling of pride as if I had been a real guide at The Homestead. In addition, I learned some things, including how the historical legacies were transmitted to the people who visit, the guiding program's backbone, and actual procedures. The group was divided into two. One group was led by a regular tour guide, and the other was led by myself. When the tour ended at the doorstep, I realized that I had spent much more time than a tour would usually take. I put more into my presentation because I had been afraid that they might have been disappointed by having a Japanese tour guide. They asked me questions and I was glad that I had encouraged them in their interest in Dickinson. The following day, I ran into a Japanese girl who introduced herself as one of the group members from the day before. We talked for some time about Dickinson and she said she was eager to know more about her. She added that the group members had talked about how my enthusiasm had impressed them. This discovery made my experience even more rewarding. It was a revelation to know that I could really work in this regard for Emily. I want a great many people to have the opportunity to get to know her and her work. I constantly strive to act as a sort of agent for her, and receiving that type of feedback gave me valuable encouragement that I was on the right track.

In 2004, I returned again to Amherst for a short visit and I found that The Homestead and The Evergreens were combined into one entity now known as the Emily Dickinson Museum — a feat that had been accomplished through the wonderful collaboration of the two directors of each house. Now, a single admission to the museum permits a tour of both houses. The Homestead's red brick was being painted ochre — a return to its period color. The Todd's house (The Dell) had been renovated into a bed-and-breakfast and some of Mabel Todd's artifacts had been brought there from the Amherst Historical Society.

Almost twenty years have passed since I first came to Amherst. Several familiar faces were now gone — some moved away from Amherst, some forever. One old friend had disappeared — the giant katsura tree in front of Grace Episcopal Church that had been brought by William Clark from Japan was gone. Disease and old age made it a hazard and it had to be cut down. Speaking of Clark, a new theory by Ruth Jones, a local historian, has been circulating that he might have been the person Emily referred to as her master. Even though people and trees might disappear some new interpretation of, or speculation on, Emily always crops up.

During this last visit I saw a dance performance at Jacob's Pillow, which is an hour or so drive into the Berkshires from Amherst. I began to talk with a woman who sat next to me. She told me that her friend had written a play titled *Eastward to Eden*, which was based on Emily's life. Its first performance was also during the time of *A Streetcar Named Desire*'s first run on Broadway. I read *Eastward to Eden* when I returned later to the Jones Library. The book contained several pictures of the play's first performance, which reminded me exactly of the movie version of *Little Women*. That new information made me recall something very familiar — what's new evokes the old and what's old is seen in a new light. Emily always plays that magic on me, charming me as I meditate on the endless divagations of the mysteries of time.

# Epilogue

During my first stay in Amherst in from 1986 to 1987, every day was packed with things that filled me with amazement and wonder. It seemed a pity to keep all that I had experienced to myself. My stay had been made possible by the Japanese Ministry of Education and it was strongly suggested that I should bring back something not only for me, but for my fellow Japanese to contemplate. In light of this obligation, I set to work recording my life in the United States. Finding time to do so with such a busy schedule was not easy. Once I returned to Japan, it was almost impossible to find time to finish the writing and the editing. I struggled to fill in the gaps, and to sort out what I had already written in the United States.

Even before I left in 1987, I knew that I would return. Luckily, nearly seven years later I came back to Amherst for a year through the American Council of Learned Scholars (ACLS) and Osaka Shoin Women's University, the institution for which I now work. I felt as if I had something to finish. And I thought my stay would be somewhat meaningless unless I completed recording my experiences. I firmly resolved to finish the book that was to incorporate my experiences from both trips.

During my second stay, I was often asked by my American friends and acquaintances why I was here. My answer was, "To do research and to write a book." They would inquire further, "Is the book going to be in English?" I answered, "No way. Of course, not." The book had to be written in Japanese since the ministry wanted me to deliver something that would benefit the Japanese public. But I was asked this question so often that I began to entertain the idea of writing both in Japanese and English. I knew very well that this would be a nearly impossible, so I was extremely hesitant. But so many people encouraged me that I decided to give it a try.

However, just as I had anticipated, the task involved the heavy burden of language and translation issues. And I now had to finish two books instead of just one. My resolve certainly wavered. Struggling with the intense pressure, I somehow managed to finish writing in both Japanese and English and returned home. I published *Emiri no Shi no Ie (Emily's House of Poetry)* in Japan in 1996. Editing it took a considerable amount of time since in my enthusiasm I had written twice as much as was needed.

To finish and to edit my English book, I absolutely needed to spend another long stay in the United States, which seemed almost impossible. Since there are no sabbaticals, per se, in Japan, few professors can leave their teaching posts for long periods. I had already taken two very long leaves — one in my former position at Mie University and one in my new job at Osaka Shoin Women's University. I nearly gave up.

Somehow fate brought me to the Osaka American Center to visit a Japanese man who was in charge of the department of public relations and cultural exchange there. He had lived and worked in the United States for a number of years. We talked for nearly an hour about the relationship of Japan and the United States, the future of Japan, and living abroad. At the end, he told me, "I think you'd be happier living there." Taken aback, I protested, "No, no. I love Japan too much. I don't think of myself as particularly patriotic, but in the United States, I find myself much more so. When I'm there, I discover my Japanese identity while, at the same time, I learn and appreciate American ways." He understood. He replied, "What I mean is that you can follow your heart in the United States." That, I could not deny. Then, he handed me a packet — a complete set of application materials for a Fulbright. When I looked into it, I discovered that there was an age limit ("preferably candidates are under fifty-five"); I was just barely eligible. Since

*Epilogue*

I knew that the competition would be fairly steep, I hesitated to apply. And I knew very little about the examination process. Yet, I felt guilty not following up this man's kind suggestion. I decided to apply and I left everything to luck.

After it was announced that I was an award recipient, my school let me study abroad again. Thus, I came back to Amherst in 2000 for seven months, to write most of what became *this* book.

**quale** [kwa-lay]. *Eng.* n 1. A property (such as hardness) considered apart from things that have that property. 2. A property that is experienced as distinct from any source it may have in a physical object. *Ital.* pron.a. 1. Which, what. 2. Who. 3. Some. 4. As, just as.